BLITHE SPIRITS

BLITHE SPIRITS

A TOAST TO THE COCKTAIL BY JILL SPALDING

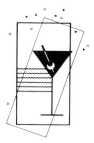

PHOTOGRAPHY BY
JESSE GERSTEIN AND MARK DANIELS

ALVIN ROSENBAUM PROJECTS, INC., WASHINGTON, D. C.

Blithe Spirits, A Toast to the Cocktail

Editors: Leonard Sherp and Nancy L. Johnson
Designer: Kathleen Mary Hardesty

Library of Congress Cataloguing in Publication Data

Spalding, Jill.
   Blithe spirits.

   Includes index
   1. Cocktails. I. Title.
TX951.S66 1988   641.8'74   88-22199
ISBN 0-87491-915-0

Printed in the United States of America

CONTENTS

ACKNOWLEDGMENTS

The history of the cocktail is strewn with mythology, apochryphal tales, unfounded claims and exaggeration. Dozens of people helped to verify the origin of drinks and provided stories, anecdotes, leads and sources. Countless bartenders, trusty keepers of the lore, responded graciously and readily to my seemingly endless inquiries and requests for information; I thank them all from the bottom of many a glass. Alice Gross, manager of library services at Joseph E. Seagram & Sons in New York, combed her shelves for appropriate background reading. Nancy Johnson, research director at Alvin Rosenbaum Projects, always seemed able to discover even the most arcane piece of information in a flash.

Baccarat generously provided crystal for the photography. The Seagram Museum, Waterloo, Ontario, supplied labels and other materials. Usha Singh of Club El Morocco in New York opened her picture files. The Hotel Bel Air in Los Angeles hosted the production team in comfort and style; the entire staff, especially Paul Zuest, manager, and Kevin Kaeff, bar manager did everything possible to make the work there go smoothly.

Photography and design of Blithe Spirits was directed by Kathleen Hardesty; the striking beauty of this book is tribute of its own. Aaron Rosenbaum and Adobe Systems, Inc. were helpful in the production of the book using a Macintosh™ desktop publishing system.

My final thanks go to Alvin Rosenbaum, my publisher, and Leonard Sherp, my editor. Without Alvin, this book would never have been started; without Leonard, it might never have been completed.

TEXAS FIZZ

A Texas Fizz is a Gin Fizz Texas-style, substituting grenadine and champagne for sugar syrup and soda water. Combine a tablespoon of grenadine, two teaspoons of orange juice and one and one-half shots of gin in a shaker. Shake vigorously, and pour into a tall glass with ice. Top with champagne.

INTRODUCTION

"We are the pilgrims of our own celebration."
—Max Gerard

Was there life before spirit? One would be hard pressed to prove it, so endemic to the well-being of the earliest societies was their felicitous relationship with fermentation.

Cocktails, of course, are a more recent invention, though not as contemporary as commonly held, convention having placed the earliest confections correctly in America but less accurately in the turbulent lap of the 1920s.

In reality, the first cocktails saw the dawn sometime around the turn of the nineteenth century and worked their way decorously into every cranny of American life, reaching a pinnacle of dizzying prominence during Prohibition and the years immediately following. Left to languish in the sobering times of the Depression and a second World War, the cocktail was gratefully revived by executives and hostesses, reigned happily for a decade at business luncheons and cocktail parties, then nearly retired when it failed to enchant a generation newly drawn to the pale nicety of white wine before dinner.

Intriguingly, if not entirely unexpectedly, the cocktail is fashionable again, partly as a lark, partly as a serious contributor to the art of fine living, as its legendary versatility is adapting a wide variety of mixed drinks to new standards of fitness, moderation and very high style. In tune with the times, news columns now trumpet the cocktail's grand comeback with such headlines as "Martini Redux," "Stocks Are Down, Gin Is Back," and "The Manhattan Is It!" and relate its return to current trends towards gourmet refinement and novel amusement.

More to the point is that cocktails are no longer primarily about drink. They are about style and atmosphere and social interaction. In today's stylish world, there is greater interest in the aesthetic, the ornamental. There are more occasions to dress up for, to dress up food and drink for. The eighties are a synthesis of layers and colors and textures and moods upon which life itself is built up like a vivid Pousse Cafe.

Committed to only the best, people are returning to excellence, asking of liquid ingredients the same quality and visual appeal as of foodstuffs. With a heightened appreciation of artful detail, people are discovering that there is a good deal more to mixing a drink than upending liquor over ice cubes.

The modern world has shifted priorities, moving purposefully in the direction of health and the good life. Drinking remains in the mainstream of American life, but with a new understanding of how to relate alcohol to physical well-being. The inclination to moderation and nutrition is stimulating fruitful experimentation with liquor, making cocktails look very modern and very good again.

The contemporary drinker, mindful of health but dedicated to style, committed to moderation but interested in novelty, has discovered that somewhere between the robust taste of straight whiskey and the blandness of wine spritzers is a world of delectable distillations that can be sweet or spicy, tall or short, nutritionally light but seductively flavorful. Wine may be genteel, but cocktails are more fun, more romantic, more celebratory and even, when properly prepared, more elegant.

What has facilitated the cocktail's revival is that unlike other period artworks like the Tiffany lamp and the T-Bird, it is easily reinvented. The mold is not broken, the die has not melted. Superb spirits, bottled mixers and fresh juices are delicacies available to everyone. With a recipe, ingredients available for the buying, fresh ice and an appropriate glass, the cocktail can be restored to its full glory at the twirl of a swizzle stick.

As the modern drinker, like finely-aged whiskey, matures in attitude and taste, so, too, is the cocktail experiencing a coming of age, taking its place among the foremost pleasures of this world. The old-time bars remain friendly faces in the crowd, their barkeeps the guardians of arcane recipes and the purveyors of rare liquids, but the home and its extensions, the backyard and the picnic-ground, have become the hearth-stones of creative confections.

The cocktail hour is now an international tradition as, in that suspended moment between work and dinner, people all over the world stop to enjoy a good drink. The cocktail itself has expanded gastronomic expectations with the awareness of how many sensations, how much pungent pleasure can be called up by the fireside in the circumference of a glass—the fragrances of summer locked in a snifter, the lore of Scotland moored in a rocks glass, the romance of the South suspended for one perfect moment in a frosted silver tumbler—all indelibly contributing to the complete sense of well-being a good drink can provide. The aroma, the taste and the atmosphere it creates stimulate the appetite, charm the senses and ease the transition from day into night.

BLITHE SPIRITS

"The future of American thought, poetry, and religion
—the future of the American world—is intimately
interwoven with whiskey sours."
—Delmore Schwartz

"Cocktails, please, Saunders," cried a character from one of Noel Coward's early plays. She was, of course, a bright young thing, bubbling in the champagne glass of the 1920s, to whom all the world was cocktails and all its men and women blithe imbibers. Never had mixed drinking seen merrier times than in those bibulous days in America when Prohibition cancelled inhibition and launched a roller coaster of easy money seeking instant fun. As the nation progressed from a melting pot to a cocktail shaker, drinks were ordered for their colors and the curiosity of their names—Pink Ladies, Fur Collars, Angel Tits—with caution counting little and discernment not at all. So entrenched was the cocktail in Jazz-Age America, so generic to its lifestyle, that it now seems part of our heritage, like turkey, like cake.

In fact, the cocktail has not been around a very long time. Spirits, of course, have been with us since the gods first cast man off to seek his own stimulation. The word "alcohol" itself derives from the ancient Arabic *al kohl*. Distillation was practiced by the early Egyptians, fermentation made manifest in the Bible, and the aperitif craze, according to Pliny, originated in Rome in the reign of Tiberius. "Bacchus opens the gate of the heart," observed Horace, and down through the ages the bards have attested to his insight in verses that are nothing if not heartfelt. "Give me some aqua vitae," cries Shakespeare's Falstaff; "Fill the goblet again for I never before/ Felt the glow that now gladdens my heart to its core," sang Lord Byron. How much greater their inspiration might have been had they savored their muse in its most sublime incarnation can be

GIN RICKEY

A Rickey is any mixed drink made with spirits, lime and carbonated water. This effervescent 1895 creation was named for Colonel Joe Rickey, a Washington, D.C. imbiber who was certainly its champion, if not its inventor.

The popular Gin Rickey is made by combining two ounces of gin and the juice and rind of one small lime over ice in a highball glass. Top with carbonated water, and serve with a swizzle stick. Since the Gin Rickey is a dry drink, many prefer to sweeten it with a dash of sugar syrup.

but surmised, for the cocktail was a nineteenth-century inspiration and, like the lightbulb and the refrigerator, a product of American ingenuity.

True, the liquid foundation was very much in place. Columbus had brought sugar cane to the West Indies, where the settlers took no time at all to conjure molasses into rum, and the Pilgrims put in at Plymouth Rock not for the scenery but because they had run out of beer. The Founding Fathers, too, were a spirited lot. George Washington ran a thriving whiskey distillery; Thomas Jefferson was a noted vintner. Benjamin Franklin compiled and published a dictionary of drinking terms. Samuel Adams was a brewer's son, Patrick Henry a tavern keeper, and John Hancock joined John Adams in the fight against the rum tax.

In that colonial era of contaminated water and inclement weather, liquor was virtually mandatory and as respectable as coat tails. Certainly, according to an historian of the day, there was no occasion—birth, wedding, contract or funeral—that took place without spirits: "No farm hand in haying, no sailor on a vessel, no worker in a mill, no cobbler, tailor, carpenter, mason or tinker would work without some strong drink."

What wasn't provided on the job was procured at the inn. The tavern was the town hall of its day, where citizens met over a cheering cup to hold trials, draft resolutions and even pass laws. America's destiny was forged in taverns. Revolutionary fervor drew its resolve from The Red Inn; the Indian Queen Tavern gave birth to the Declaration of Independence; and it was at Fraunces Tavern that General Washington delivered his farewell address to his troops.

Quite understandably, the Crown's ill-advised tax on beverage alcohol stuck fast in the colonists' gullets. Spirits, they said, were none of Britain's damn business. Gin had come over with the Dutch, whisky with the Scots and rum with God. It was this resolve of the colonials to defend life, liberty and the pursuit of liquor that helped to ignite the earliest uprisings that led to the War for Independence.

Arguably, however, it was a far more revolutionary gesture when some inspired citizen of the New World first chose to toss one of these "strong waters" around with another. Exactly who this creative mixologist was remains as much of a mystery as the origin of the word "cocktail" itself, which was first used in a Maryland diary in 1806 to describe a "stimulating liquor composed of spirits of any kind, sugar, water and bitters." One legend has it that shady traders fed their horses whiskey to make them cock their tails prettily for prospective buyers, another that it derives from "cock's ale," a spiked brew distributed at cockfights. More colorful is James Fenimore Cooper's assertion that a spirited barmaid, Betsy Flanagan, stirred the rum bracers she served to the Revolutionary officers with tailfeathers plucked from the rooster of a neighboring Tory. Most plausible is its attribution to Antoine Peychaud, an eighteenth-century New Orleans apothecary who dispensed fortifying brandy tonics in double-ended egg cups, or *coquetiers*.

The early cocktails were haphazard brews, prepared in the manner of potions and administered or taken throughout a winter day much as an elixir or an extra blanket. More elaborate concoctions, such as the famous Schuylkill's Fish House Punch, which dates back to 1732, and the orgeats and brandy

cordials detailed in Mrs. Randolph's recipe book of 1828, accompanied ceremonials and high festivities. Even cocktails *per se* were flourishing by 1839, when Captain Marryat noted in the journal of his travels that "the Americans do not confine themselves to foreign wines or liquors; they have every variety at home, in the shape of compounds, such as mint-julep and its variations; slings in all their varieties; cocktails."

The next three decades witnessed the invention of other "modern" cocktails—the Tom Collins, the Brandy Sour and the Rickey—but there was no separate ritual, no pre-prandial hour set aside for enjoying a mixed drink, until some enlightened moment of the later nineteenth century. Perhaps the planet warmed, or machinery took the hardship from the working day, or perhaps the first recruits to America's loose-limbed fast set resented standing stiffly about before dinner. Prohibition clinched the matter, calling on all the depths of Yankee resourcefulness to confound the law with exotic concoctions consumed in the privacy of one's parlor before stepping out for a night on the blue-law town.

England took more slowly to the whole idea. No slouches at drinking, as attested to by the notorious eighteenth-century gin palaces of London's East End and accounts of dinners as liquid as those of Galsworthy's Forsytes, who quaffed sherry, champagne, port and brandy at a single sitting, the Victorians nonetheless preferred to keep their liquors separated from each other and attached to meals. Even the racier Edwardians made little headway in relieving *le mauvais quart d'heure*, that interminable interval between a punctua arrival and the announcement of dinner, with a little something alcoholic.

It took the Jazz-Age insouciance of expatriate socialites and headstrong heiresses like Laura Corrigan and Nancy Cunard to introduce English youth to the charms of a Mint Julep. Contagion was immediate. The froth and the fun of it suited perfectly the transition from waltz time to the quick step of the 1920s, and the era of the cocktail in Europe was launched.

Back home, the tempo of American drinking had accelerated. "Never were there such parties!" wrote young David Niven; "Never such gaiety," fluted pied piper Elsa Maxwell. "Cocktail," according to C. K. Ogden's *The System of Basic English*, was among the fifty best-known words in the English language—two others on the list being "alcohol" and "bar." "Drink and gossip with Tallulah," read an entry in Coward's diary; "We splashed about and drank rum and picnicked," read another. And several entries later: "I sat on the verandah watching the sunset, sipping a whiskey and reflecting on life…"

Now as then, when held against the moonlight, balanced on the railing beneath a Caribbean sunset or placed beside another on a table set for two, the cocktail reflects the spectrum of well-being: the cheer of Christmas, the toast of friendship, the surrender of a holiday, the promise of the New Year and every shade of feeling in between. In that velvet hour of evening when candles twinkle in the Baccarat and even Angostura glitters, in that lilting moment when a silver shaker, a frosted tumbler and a rose in fluted crystal beguile the senses, then is it revealed to the low and the mighty, who have rubbed elbows forever along the mahogany of the world's famous bars, that spiritous liquids are capital assets and that this nation's finest hour is its Happy Hour.

20

AQUAE VITAE

"It ain't tea."

—Sarah Gamp in Charles Dickens' *Martin Chuzzlewit*

What is a cocktail? "The sweetest form of alchemy," said Lord Rothschild. "A longer word for joy," enthused Clara Bow. "The world in a glass," chirped a Duchess of Devonshire. To the American designer Valentina it was "style on a stem"; to W. H. Auden it was "a solace in old age"; to the less reverent Ogden Nash, "a tingle remarkably pleasant."

A cocktail, one might conclude, is what one perceives it to be. Loosely, it's a pretty froth; compactly, it's distilled ambrosia. Mentally it's a tonic, artfully it's a creation, casually it's a concoction. Aesthetically, it is the essence of style.

Generically and technically, however, a cocktail is any mixed drink made with one or more spirits in combination with water, ice, other beverages or flavorings that derive either from produce—cucumbers, oranges, celery, lemons—known affectionately as "garbage," or from groceries—cream, ice-cream, soup—viewed less tolerantly as nonsense.

The nitty gritty, of course, is alcohol, itself a product of alchemy, though of humble and ubiquitous origins in that spirits can be wrought from virtually anything: rum from molasses, applejack from cider, brandy from grapes, gin and whiskey from grain, vodka from potatoes, tequila from cactus and aquavit from sawdust.

The trick—and the skill—is the process, the centuries of technique and tippling that have gone into the distilling, infusing and fermenting of the liquors of today. The fun of a cocktail may be the fizz and the ornaments, but its heart and its soul are the spirits.

DAIQUIRI

The Daiquiri was conceived in 1915, when two engineers from Bethlehem Steel found themselves in the midst of a malaria epidemic in the village of Daiquirí, near Santiago, Cuba. They began putting a little rum in their boiled drinking water as a disinfectant. That brew lacked flavor, so they added a bit of lime, then a touch of sugar. When possible, they added ice made from distilled water and soon found the concoction pleasurable as well as medicinal.

A regular Daiquiri is made by combining one and a half shots of rum, a shot of lime juice and a teaspoon of super-fine sugar in an ice-filled shaker. Shake, and strain into a cocktail glass; garnish with a wedge of lime. Frozen Daiquiris are made by combining the ingredients of a Daiquiri with crushed ice in a blender, with fresh fruit often added for even more flavor.

There is no mystery about this most gregarious of liquors other than the origin of its name; from "rumbustion," perhaps, old English for the rumpus caused by intemperate sailors. A more likely derivation is from the Latin *saccharum*, meaning sweet, since the Spaniards, via Columbus—who brought the first sugar cane cuttings from the Canary Islands—and Ponce de León—who established himself lucratively as Puerto Rico's initial sugar king—were the first distillers in the Caribbean.

One of the most versatile and most fragrant of all spirits, rum is also one of the simplest to make. Molasses formed from the clarified extract of sugar cane is left to ferment with its valued impurities, then is transformed into rum by as many as three distillations. As the rum ages in the barrel, coloring is enhanced by adding caramel to darken or by filtering through charcoal to lighten. The rums are then tasted and expertly blended for more individual flavor. The whole process takes three years or more, though rum may continue to improve in oak casks for twenty years.

The early stuff was crude, a "hot, hellish and terrible spirit" called "kill-devil," which was used largely to pacify the slaves working the plantations of St. Croix. The first potable version was distilled in the Colonies and established many a great American fortune by its infamous role in the "slave triangle": slaves to the Caribbean, sugar cane to New England, rum to Africa. It made good ballast for trading ships returning empty to England and prime booty for pirates, who further fueled

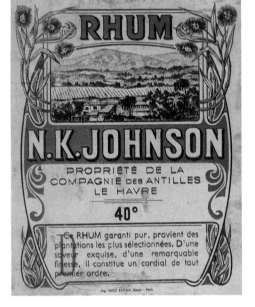

their swashbuckling ventures from copper stills stashed between Jamaica and Barbados.

Other satisfied customers were Her Majesty's sailors, thanks to Samuel Pepys, who, as secretary of the Admiralty, authorized generous rations before battle. The ensuing skirmishes were lively but disastrous, until Edward Vernon, nicknamed "Old Grog" for his rough grogram coat, diluted the rations with water and, to stave off scurvy, with lime juice—an inspiration that tagged all British as limeys and coincided with the resounding defeat of the Spanish at the Battle of Cartagena. Vernon was instantly promoted to Admiral, and his dilution made such headway in working class life that in time "grog" became the word for all liquor. It was illegal, however, for the English to make rum, and it would be well into the eighteenth century before the upper classes condescended to exchange it for brandy and whisky in their ubiquitous punches.

By then, rum had established its stronghold in colonial America, largely for economic reasons, being so cheap and reliable a substitute for liquors made from the more seasonal sources of fructose and glucose. Home brews still cheered, but rum proved more effective against the rigors of the frontier. Children were served it in their porridge, and in the South a nip at breakfast was conveniently believed to stave off malaria.

During the Revolutionary War, one of the first acts of the newly-independent state of New Hampshire was to designate rum as a "Necessary and Convenient Article of Life." General Washington, who had won election to his first term in the Virginia House of Burgesses after distributing seventy-five gallons

CUBA LIBRE

Since Castro's takeover, it is improbable that the real thing finds its way into Havana cocktail hours with any frequency. But the Cuba Libre, better known in the U.S. as a Rum and Coke with a lime, remains popular everywhere from the backyard to the nightclub because of its sweet, refreshing simplicity.

Over ice in a highball or collins glass, combine one large jigger of light rum and the juice of one small lime. Fill with cola, and garnish with a wedge of lime.

of the spirit among his constituents, remained loyal to its cause, badgering the Commissary for supplies for his army and rewarding good soldiering with extra rations.

After Independence, however, rum fell afoul of politics. A tax favoring production of Kentucky bourbon sent rum into a decline that lasted more than a century, until its resurrection in the 1920s into the world of the cocktail, as vacationers returning from tropical getaways brought back the first exotic rum drinks: Daiquiris, Mai Tais and Jamaica's famous Planter's Punch, whose colorful fruit and paper umbrellas became props in the fantasy decor of bar stops like Don The Beachcomber and, later, Trader Vic's.

Rum soared in popularity in the sixties, when the new interest in lighter-flavored drinks drew attention to Puerto Rico's white varieties, so amenable to frothy interpretations like the Piña Colada and the Daisy, while the darker rums found a permanent home in the cool, summer punches of warm weather playgrounds and the cheering hot toddies of winter mountain resorts.

The Old Fashioned was first mixed at the Pendennis Club in Louisville for one Colonel James E. Pepper, a distiller of bourbon whiskey. The bartender placed a cube of sugar in a short glass and sprinkled it with a dash of Angostura bitters. He then added a little soda water and stirred, an act which came to be known as muddling. After muddling, he poured in a jigger or two of bourbon, added a few ice cubes and garnished with both a slice of lemon and a maraschino cherry. Adaptations call for a slice of orange or a squirt of soda water. An Old Fashioned should be served with a swizzle stick.

"Freedom and Whisky gang thegither!" — Robert Burns

When David Niven went off to the front in World War II, Clark Gable cautioned him: "Stick to Scotch if you want to be brave, gin only makes you piss."

An Irishman would endorse the spirit of this advice, but emend it to "whiskey," planting the flag of its origin squarely in Ireland. Credit for its invention goes to Irish monks, who first snatched the secret of distillation out of Europe, then substituted a grain base for grapes in deference to the climate. They must have been well into the production of their *uisce beathadh* by the eleventh century, because a chronicle of that time, the ancient *Book of Leinster*, records the revels of a merry band who "partook of it heartily" at the Monastery of Dundadheen, set out for the East Coast and woke the next morning all the way to the south in the County of Limerick. Adding credence to the Irish claim is the fact that the "Old Bushmills" Distillery in Ireland's County Antrim was the first ever to be licensed by the Crown, in 1608, and therefore claims to be the world's oldest whiskey distillery.

Fiddlesticks, cry the Scots. Scotch isn't "whiskey," it's "whisky," and it's ours. The first *properly* rectified spirit, they insist, was distilled in the monasteries of the Highlands sometime in the fifteenth century by the well-documented procedure, still used today, that gives each of Scotland's single malts its inimitable flavor. First the barley is malted, then dried over an open flame, with peat providing smoke that adds flavor and aroma to the eventual spirit. The malted barley is then mixed with hot water to make a sweet liquid called "wort," to which yeast is added for fermentation. The resulting elixir is distilled

twice in giant pot stills, then matured in oak casks where it must age for at least three years to be called Scotch whisky. Obviously, say the Scots, the earlier Irish versions were nothing at all in comparison, and to underscore their differences, they shortened their *uisge beatha* to "whisky," dropping the "e" to distinguish it forever.

Scotch whisky would remain a local treasure until 1746, when the inaccessible Highlands were opened to trade by England's triumph at the Battle of Culloden. Even then the English remained loyal to brandy until the late 1860s, when phylloxera sailed over from America to decimate Europe's vineyards. With the supply of their beloved brandy so drastically curtailed, the British discovered the enchantment of whisky, a turn made more readily acceptable by the recent introduction of the continuous still, which enabled the production of lighter-flavored, blended Scotches that enjoyed a wider following and gave whisky the popularity the Scots had long thought its due.

Americans, on the other hand, knew a good thing when they met it. Whiskey emigrated early to the New World, distilled originally from rye by the Scotch-Irish settlers in the Shenandoah Valley. Alexander Hamilton's egregious tax of 1791 that triggered the Whiskey Rebellion accelerated a migration to then-remote Kentucky, where the new distillations, known as "moonshine" or "mountain dew," were being made from more plentiful maize and water from limestone-filtered springs as pure as those of Scotland. From "them thar hills" came bourbon, its origin popularly credited to a minister from Bourbon County, Kentucky, the Reverend Elijah Craig,

to whom it had been revealed in 1789, the same year that George Washington became president, that whiskey aged in a barrel that he had accidentally charred verged on sublimity.

Bourbon straight up became the drink that first separated America's men from its boys and the birthright of all southerners. The closest it came to the mixed drink was Bourbon and "Branch," southern for small stream. Northerners were less

purist. The cargo of a riverboat destined for Montana which sank in the Mississippi River in 1865 held five thousand gallons of whiskey, champagne and schnapps—and twenty kegs of "bourbon cocktail."

Within a year of this celebrated capsize, whiskeys were being bottled and advertised in mail-order catalogues. Brand names were established, becoming a more effective selling point than price. One "Special Introductory Offer" threw in a grandfather clock, a five-hundred pound safe or a cash register with the purchase of twenty-six two-dollar gallons of Rock and Rye.

Once whiskey took hold as the nation's preferred drink, Americans became selective. Of the two domestic styles, straight and blended, blends being made up of a combination of whiskeys, they favored the blends and, after Prohibition had brought them to America's attention, their northern counterparts, the Canadian whiskies.

Inevitably, whiskey's high visibility made it Prohibition's main target, so it went underground, put on pretty disguises and surfaced to join the cocktail parade as the Rusty Nail, the Rob Roy and the Old Fashioned. Bourbon retained pride of place with the Manhattan and the Mint Julep, but the blends eventually stole the show, with Seven and Seven—Seagram's Seven Crown and Seven-Up—entering the eighties as America's most popular mixed drink.

SEVEN AND SEVEN

Seven and Seven, long one of the most popular cocktails in America, is made with Seagram's Seven Crown, a blend of seven whiskies, and Seven-Up, hence the name. Variations allow for the substitution of other lemon-lime sodas, but the smooth, blended flavor of Seven Crown is indispensable.

Over ice in a highball or collins glass, add a jigger or more of whisky, and fill with Seven-Up. The very adaptable Seven and Seven is delicious and appropriate before, during and after a meal.

MARTINI COCKTAIL

CLOVER LEAF COCKTAIL

BRONX COCKTAIL

MUCH BETTER WHEN MADE OF GORDON!

"Truth should be like a gin twist, half and half." — Nineteenth-century English adage

Once the soporific of the masses, now the soul of the hallowed Martini, gin was invented around 1650 in Holland by a chemist at the University of Leiden, whose search for a diuretic led to the combining of the medicinal juniper berry with a clear, grain-based spirit. The resultant *genever* was a palpable hit with the pocketbook as well as the palate, since it derived from a source that was abundant and cheap, relative to the fruit bases of other contemporary alcohols, and could be consumed immediately on production, being one of the few spirits of that time that did not require aging. Refinements would come later with the addition of botanicals like cassia, anise, coriander and angelica, which varied with each label, but it was the generic *genever* that became the soldier's badge of Dutch courage and passed across the battlefields to the British, who shortened its name and compromised its reputation.

A wild move on the part of William of Orange to annihilate the brandy trade of the hated French by encouraging domestic distillation of gin made it so available that by 1743 a population of over six million was downing eighteen million gallons of such nefarious adulterations as "My Lady's Eyewash." In the name of gin, cheap flavored-alcohols were peddled on street corners and in chandeliered saloons, to gentlemen, to prisoners, to ladies who shopped.

Once purified and standardized by a multiple distillation process into unsweetened London Dry Gin—thus distinguishing it from the sweet Old Tom Gin and the original Holland's, whose single distillation from mash produces a maltier flavor best enjoyed on the rocks—gin climbed to its pedestal as the Englishman's preferred spirit, mainstay of the original Pimm's Cup and boon companion to Italian vermouth in the famed Gin and It.

Sometime before the airship, London Dry Gin crossed the Atlantic, where it quickly usurped the domain of the domestic variety—a fixture since Dutch colonists established the first distillery in New Amsterdam—and climbed to complete respectability in such celebrated cocktails as the Clover Club, the Horse's Neck, the Gimlet and the immortal Martini.

"Vodka is the *only* drink." — Diana Vreeland

Exalting in the deadpan, the quintessence of neutrality, American vodka is the character actor of the spirits. By law it is processed to lack all distinction—no aroma, no taste—befitting it more for combining with other flavors than for drinking straight up.

The original vodka was an entirely different story, a tale of peasants and kings, first created from a rye base sometime in the twelfth century, probably in Russia, possibly in Poland, and almost certainly for medicinal purposes, as a crude spirit called *zhiznennia voda*, "water of life."

By the eighteenth century, cherished by its diminutive, "little water," vodka was being distilled throughout the Russian Empire from barley, maize or, more popularly, potatoes. The type that eventually travelled to the West is of the grain-based Petrovskaya variety, named for Peter the Great, who perfected its distillation process with information gained from his incognito sojourn in Holland. It was meant for drinking straight up: "*Prosit vodka*," Boris Pasternak used to call it, meaning a full glass per toast and count the boots under the table the next morning.

That the appeal of vodka came late to the West is clearly evidenced by Captain Horatio Hornblower's perilous initiation at the court of the Czar, so vividly recounted by E. M. Forster in his novel of that name. "That is caviar," the Countess explained to him, "and this is vodka, the drink of the people, but I think you will find that the two are admirably suited to each other." He did, and she did, and honor was saved only by the ending of the chapter.

SALTY DOG
The Screwdriver of the fifties became the Greyhound in the seventies when grapefruit juice was substituted for orange juice, vodka remaining the constant. Rimming the glass with rock salt makes the Greyhound a Salty Dog.

Over ice in a tall glass rimmed with salt, combine grapefruit juice and a shot and a half of vodka.

39

MOSCOW MULE

Unlike most cocktails, invented through careful experimentation with cherished ingredients, the popular Moscow Mule's birth was purely a business matter. A bartender at Los Angeles' Cock and Bull Restaurant attempted to rid himself of a lingering supply of ginger beer by combining it with vodka and lime juice, and serving it in a copper mug as a novelty.

Over ice in a now-traditional copper mug, combine a shot of vodka and the juice of half a lime. Fill mug with ginger beer or ginger ale, and garnish with a slice of cucumber or a wedge of lime.

The French, enamoured of their *rhum* and their wines, acknowledged vodka even later. It was well into the 1950s when Pablo Picasso, asked to list the most important new features of post-war France, named modern jazz, Brigitte Bardot and Polish vodka.

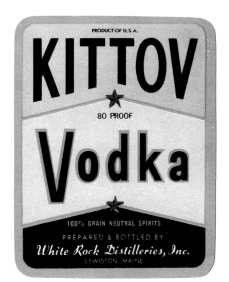

Like the French, Americans remained completely uninterested until after World War II, apart from a few of the more widely travelled who enjoyed the party trick of tossing back both the spirits and their glasses. Then, one fateful June day in 1946, a bartender from The Cock and Bull in Los Angeles decided to rid himself of an overstock of ginger beer. Unsuccessful attempts to mix in whiskey and gin led to the last ditch attempt of vodka and lime juice. Out of such chemistry was the Moscow Mule born, heralding a new chapter in the history of the cocktail and a revolution in the production of vodka. Hitherto unknown Russian vodkas were hastily imported and adopted immediately by professionals with a predilection for something rare on the rocks. Indeed, "Stoli on ice" retained executive privilege until the Soviet invasion of Afghanistan switched America's affection to Sweden's Absolut.

But it was the newly-created American vodkas, tasteless and odorless, that climbed most readily into bed with all the fruits of the earth to produce the Bloody Mary, the Screwdriver, the Greyhound, the Cape Codder and all the other well-behaved confections that were thought to leave no hangovers and tell no tales out of school.

BLITHE SPIRIT
What better way to toast the return of the cocktail than with the invention of a new cocktail. The Blithe Spirit partakes of classic ingredients from spirits' glorious past—brandy, Cointreau and champagne—and mixes them with two contemporary favorites, cranberry juice and passion fruit juice.

In a champagne flute, combine equal parts of brandy, passion fruit juice and cranberry juice, and a splash of Cointreau. Top with champagne to fill, and garnish with a fresh strawberry.

"You can have too much champagne to drink, but you can never have enough." — Elmer Rice

A wine, yes, but so popular is champagne for combining with fruit, so generic were its bubbles to the giggles of the Jazz Age, and so emblematic does it remain for all contemporary celebration that champagne is traditionally an item on every mixed-drink list.

Refreshingly, its provenance is precise, the *domaine* of Champagne near Rheims in France, whose inhabitants had discovered that by leaving their wine to ferment a second time in the spring, they could transform it into a sparkling delicacy. But it was only in the 1600s that the Benedictine monk Dom Pérignon developed the *méthode champagnoise,* through his discovery that the blending of wines from several vineyards produced a wine greater than any of its components. He is also credited with first using a cork stopper resistant to pressure, making it practical to embark on the complex procedure of converting sparkling wine to champagne that has come down to us today.

In the spring, after the grapes are pressed and fermented, the cellarmaster decides whether to treat the new wine as a single vintage or a blend. A blend, or *cuvée,* may be skillfully compounded from as many as one hundred wines. Small amounts of yeast and sugar are added to encourage a second fermentation which produces genteel bubbles—the smaller the bubbles, say the French, the finer the champagne. The wine is bottled and left to ferment a second time for up to four years in racks tilted downward. After several years, a *remuer* so dextrous that he is able to turn thirty thousand bottles in a day

begins to twist each bottle daily to encourage the sediment shaken from the sides of the bottle to gather on the cork, which is then very carefully removed. At this delicate stage of the operation, before the second corking, the by-now sparkling wine is tailored to the preferred degree of dryness: *brut*, or dry, usually a cocktail wine; extra dry, actually sweeter than *brut* and excellent with desserts; the rarely seen *sec*, sweet rather than the dry that its name implies; or *demi-sec*, which is even sweeter. In most varieties both red and white grapes are used—the trick is to prevent the skins from contacting the juice after pressing. Because most champagne is blended from wines of different ages, the label carries no vintage, unless it has been a truly great year, one, say the growers, when the grape has had "a hundred days of sunshine." Champagnes are ready to drink when they are shipped and should be consumed within a few years after production.

It took almost no time at all for champagne to titillate England's nobility, after Charles II brought it back in his luggage from a stay in France. It found its way later to America, where it bubbled through the polite entertainments of Washington Square and Nob Hill, and frothed to the surface of the emergent society, remaining the drink of prestige and procurement throughout the Naughty Nineties, when no blade could squire a Gaiety Girl without drinking bubbly from her slipper.

Predictably, champagne dodged Prohibition to turn up at all the right places, like El Morocco and the Stork Club, as the gold-foiled symbol of affluence, liberality and post-prandial celebration. It tickled the tunes of Cole Porter and starred with Kitty Carlisle in the 1935 Broadway hit *Champagne Sea*. It was the liquid gold of our silver screen. Who can forget Garbo as Ninotchka tasting it for the first time, or Judy Holliday's dipsy malapropisms in *Born Yesterday*, or Kay Kendall's tipsy gyrations in *Genevieve*? By the 1950s champagne had become the master of all ceremonies, as predilection became custom, and custom became ritual, until no toast, no contract, no celebration seemed complete without the popping of a cork.

BELLINI

Invented at Harry's Bar in Venice in 1943, this fruity champagne cocktail was inspired by the sweet flavor of Italy's soft white peaches.

Blend five or six measures of peach nectar with a few ice cubes. Pour mixture into a Bellini glass or large goblet, and top with champagne. In season, garnish with a fresh peach slice.

With bubbly so endemic to the nation's drinking routine, with so long a chorus line getting its kicks from champagne, its transformation to a cocktail was inevitable. Regrettably, such was Americans' awe of its price and its status that their first timid efforts barely exceeded the insertion of a sugar cube, thereby surrendering their lead in elaborate concoctions to the less respectful Europeans. The Hôtel Negresco in Nice created an effervescence out of sweet champagne and precisely two strawberries, crushed. The neighboring Carlton in Cannes combined raspberries, sugar and a drop of grenadine to create the Champagne d'Amour that the chanteuse Mistinguett made popular. But the finest inspiration occurred in Venice in 1943, at the time of the retrospective of the great Venetian painter Jacopo Bellini, when Giuseppi Cipriani, owner of the already legendary Harry's Bar, combined the pulp of Italy's white summer peaches with spumante, creating, *ecco*, the Bellini. Charmed, the cocktail world replaced the sparkling wine with champagne and elevated it instantly into the pantheon of liquid delights.

Champagne on its own, served well-chilled in its *de rigueur* tulip glass, has no serious rivals, but to cultists of spiritous confections, a cocktail made with champagne remains the most urbane form of playtime, a *dalliance dangereuse* with beguiling fermentations that mingles sugar and soft fruits with dancing in the dark.

Thought to be the first spirit distilled in the Americas, tequila was already being produced by the Aztecs when the Spaniards conquered Mexico in the sixteenth century. Under a grant from the Spanish government, José Cuervo began distilling it in 1795 in the region of Jalisco, according to the formula the conquistadors had applied to the pulque that the Indians were fermenting from the heart of the agave cactus. Weighing up to 150 pounds, this vast pineapple-like core is chopped and steamed to concentrate the sap, which is then extracted and fermented twice in a copper pot-still into a powerful, clear, 106-proof mezcal. The better tequilas are aged in oak vats, Tequila Gold for two years. The very finest, called añejo, which is sought after by connoisseurs and costs the equivalent of a VSO Cognac, stays in the casks even longer, a minimum of three years.

To drink tequila as the Mexicans do requires a dextrous maneuver which calls for tossing the spirit back straight, after

first licking salt from the back of the hand and then sucking the juice from a lemon or lime. The way tequila made it over the border, however, was as grist for the cocktail mill: the glowing Tequila Sunrise, which first rose in California, and the now-classic Margarita, said to have been named by a sentimental barkeep for a young girl from Virginia City who was felled by

MARGARITA

Named for an ill-fated señorita of the Old Southwest, the Margarita has enjoyed a spirited life and recent acclaim as one of America's most popular drinks.

Like Daiquiris, Margaritas come in two forms, traditional and frozen. All Margaritas are made with a measure and a half of tequila, a measure of triple sec and half a measure of lime juice, and are served in salt-rimmed goblets.

First rub the rim of the glass, inside and out, with a wedge of lime, then dip it evenly into a saucer of rock salt. For a traditional Margarita, shake the ingredients with cracked ice, and strain the mixture into a salt-rimmed goblet or champagne saucer. For a Frozen Margarita, blend all ingredients with ice in a blender.

a stray bullet and expired in his arms. The drink has fared better, soaring to the top ten as Mexican cuisine has caught America's fancy.

Tequila had a dedicated following south of the border and in the western United States long before it became a national favorite. Even though wartime shortages of London Dry Gin in the 1940s gave tequila greater exposure, as late as 1966 food critic Craig Claiborne still felt the need to explain its charms to New Yorkers. Today cocktails made with tequila are capable of as many variations as the piñata, as Americans play around with them for their drinking amusement.

"A cocktail should be like a bugle call unto meals." — André Simon

Traditionally, an aperitif, from the Latin *aperire* meaning to open, was a drink that preceeded the main meal, awakening the palate to the forthcoming collation. For that reason, any cocktail enjoyed before dinner can be considered an aperitif, but some are more specifically intended than others to inspire interest in food. Such were the drier sherries and madeira, the wines from Spain and Portugal that found undiluted favor with the chilled gentry of English country houses.

Such, too, were the bittersweet aperitifs favored on the continent, local wines for the most part, flavored with herbs, many of which were originally bottled by medieval physicans as restoratives, digestives or nips before naps. Most popular of these wine-based elixirs is vermouth, a fortified blend of wines, matured for one year, to which as many as fifty different herbs and flowers may be added. Vermouth and its counterparts, such as Lillet, Amer Picon and Dubonnet, were long appreciated cold and with a twist of lemon; only in the last century were they extended, by combining with each other and an innovation called soda, into such summer refreshments as the Americano, an Ian Fleming favorite which became James Bond's preferred opener when on assignment in Italy.

AMERICANO

The light, effervescent Americano, favorite of Ian Fleming's James Bond in Italy, is a popular aperitif made with Campari, vermouth and soda.

Combine a shot of Campari and a shot of sweet Italian vermouth in an ice-filled highball glass. Top with soda, and garnish with a lemon twist.

BRANDY ALEXANDER

The Brandy Alexander, like many other cream cocktails, evolved from the rich egg nogs and milk punches of the Elizabethan era. Its smooth, chocolate flavor is often enjoyed as an after-dinner drink, but it is also delicious as an aperitif.

Shake equal parts brandy, crème de cacao and cream with crushed ice, and strain into a champagne saucer. Sprinkle with finely-grated nutmeg. As a prelude to a meal, add a little more brandy and a little less cream; as a dessert, rim the glass with sugar.

"Did ye iver try a brandy cocktail, Cornel?" — **William Makepeace Thackeray,** *The Newcomes*

Today the designations "cordial" and "liqueur" are interchangeable, though originally the cordial, from *cordis* meaning heart, was a cheering brew of whatever grew where—berries, damsons, angelica, what-not—saturated with sugar and infused with the spirit at hand. Simple to make and affordable, the cordial was the restorative of the populace, whereas liqueurs, which were imported distillates of some rarity, remained the post-prandials of the privileged.

Close to ten thousand brands are registered with the United States Treasury Department, which defines "cordial" as a spirit flavored with fruit, herbs, seeds or rinds, and containing at least two and one-half percent sugar.

Some liqueurs draw on the flavor of a particular spirit, Drambuie from Scotch, for example, or Grand Marnier from brandy. Many have a fruit base and thus generally rely on one of three methods to extract the delicate flavors: (1) infusion, in which the fruit or herbs are steeped in water, to which spirits are later added; (2) maceration, in which the fruit or other flavorings are soaked directly in alcohol; or (3) percolation, in which the spirit is slowly pumped through the flavoring ingredients.

Some brandies and liqueurs have strong regional followings. The French, for example, favor the heady Calvados, an apple brandy from Normandy that, even today, is often made in family-owned stills and aged up to ten years. The Swiss and Alsatians like their Poire, whose pears are sometimes grown inside bottles espaliered on the vines. The Germans swear by

Kirsch, the finest variety of which, the Schwarzwalder, is distilled from a distinctive small cherry grown in the Black Forest. The Yugoslavs enjoy Slivovitz, made with particular plums that must come from trees at least twenty years old.

Although often mentioned in the same breath with cordials, brandies are distilled directly from the fruit or the wine. Only brandy itself, as custom distinguishes the grape distillation from its sister fruit brandies, was produced in every country that made wine. The birthplace of brandy, however, is unclear. Some records trace its earliest distillation to the town of Armagnac; popular legend prefers to credit Catherine de Medici with importing it from Italy in her dowry, along with the fork and the serviette, when she married Henry II of France.

The most famous of brandies is Cognac, made only from wines grown in the Charente region of western France. The "ultimate expression of the grape," as Cognac has been hailed, is transformed from pedestrian wine to exalted spirit by a process of double distillation in flavor-trapping copper stills and years of aging in porous wood casks that allow oxygen in and alcohol vapor out. Some two million gallons are said to vanish into the air of the Charente every year; the "Angels' Share," it is called. Armagnac is another distinctive brandy, made exclusively in the Armagnac region of southwestern France.

More is known of the origins of some of the liqueurs. Most were created in specific monasteries, according to secret and arcane formulations of spices and herbs. Benedictine, which so delighted Francis I, was conjured by a monk of that order in 1521 out of twenty-eight herbs. Curaçao was distilled originally in monasteries in the Netherlands. In the seventeenth century

the Carthusian Order blended one hundred and thirty botanicals into Chartreuse, the strongest and costliest of all liqueurs, whose appeal for the finely-tuned palate verged on the mystical. In 1739 Horace Walpole made a pilgrimage to the monastery perched high in the Alps of Savoy, a daunting two-day climb by mule at the time. Almost two hundred years later Oscar Wilde tracked the yellow and green liqueurs to their source and, impressed by the monks' serenity, asked the secret of such bliss. "One-third green, two-thirds yellow," came an almoner's reply.

However, none of these ever rivalled the popularity of brandy, which found its spiritual home in England, there to reign, neat and with soda, until the vine-killing phylloxera gave whisky the lead which brandy would never reclaim. Happily, immortality was restored when brandy proved an accomplished mixer in such social combinations as the Brandy Alexander and the Brandy and Soda. Virtually all the liqueurs were recruited during Prohibition to appeal to the palates of the newly-emergent women drinkers, in such dulcet confections as the Rusty Nail, Sidecar and Between the Sheets. Today, the world's liqueurs have been vividly expanded by delectations from the Orient—melon-flavored Midori or the plum-based Aki—which have found their way into current cocktail fashion in colorful expressions like the Pink Dragon, the Green Kimono and the Rainbow Chrysanthemum.

THE ART OF THE COCKTAIL

"I never have more than one drink before dinner.
But I do like that one to be large and very strong
and very cold and very well-made."
—James Bond in Ian Fleming's *Casino Royale*

A shot of whiskey is not a cocktail. A tot of rum is not a cocktail. Soda water on an ice cube is not a cocktail. But combined in a rocks glass with a sprig of mint and a twist of lemon, they form the primitive beginnings of a Mocambo.

There is still a long way to go though, for the pitfalls of confection are unending. Is it too warm, too wet, too sweet, too flat? And how does it look?

Cocktails must be glamorous. Like birds of rare feather, they draw on more colors than the rainbow, from a palette of grenadine, crème de menthe, Curaçao and, more currently, all the mixes that are tinting spirits the day-glo colors of today's fanciful libations.

Indeed, at times cocktails have been enlisted solely for their looks. At a reception Schiaparelli gave to launch Shocking Pink, massive banquet tables that were generously swathed in her trademark color offered nothing more nourishing than the striking aesthetic of muscatel grapes and crème de menthe cocktails. On another occasion Elsa Maxwell orchestrated a ball for a rising parvenue at which every lady, upon entering, was presented with a cocktail the same color as her gown.

More memorable still was the confection designed for the *vernissage* staged by Yves Klein at the Iris Clert Gallery in 1958. The City of Paris had been persuaded to herald the opening by bathing La Concorde in blue light. The next day the entire *beaux arts* crowd, two thousand strong, turned up to find a totally empty gallery which Klein had painted white. They were allowed in

65

CREME DE MENTHE FRAPPE
Cool and bracing, a frappe is an adult version of a snowcone. The most popular is made with green crème de menthe.

Fill a cocktail glass with crushed ice, and drizzle on crème de menthe until the glass is full, about a jigger or so. Serve with a short straw.

three by three to contemplate this void, then the chosen continued on to La Coupole where they were served a special drink concocted from Curaçao and methylene. It was colorless and tasteless, but when they went home that night they peed Yves Klein blue.

But, as the saying goes, looks aren't everything. A perfectly made cocktail is a culmination of talents and, destined as it is for all the senses, a work of some complexity. It must appeal to the eye, but also taste delicious and slip down the throat, as Anna Karenina experienced it, "like tiny birds."

A cocktail is not a collectible. It is a momentary artwork, transitory, evanescent, fleeting as a mayfly. Its presentation is high theater, a masterpiece of staging, grand opera in the circumference of a goblet.

Being the most perishable of art forms, its concept and design are curatorial concerns, carefully passed down from one *afficionado* to another. Even in its heyday, when the inventing of new cocktails was America's pastime, the classic cocktail had its rules, and cultists still guard them as closely as the folios of Shakespeare. Mixing two cocktails in a large, tepid shaker is viewed as careless business; a pox on all dolts who dye ice cubes green, and the guillotine for those who shake if stirring is called for. There is simply no room in this world for a thug who bruises the gin.

Given its short chapter in the history of art, it is remarkable how many curators the cocktail has rallied to its conservation. "Never Scotch in a Manhattan," rose Faulkner's voice from the Deep South. "Banishment for the onion," thundered John Barrymore, no friend of the Gibson. "Don't mess about with

inferior ingredients," intoned Truman Capote. There have been pronouncements: "It is more important," wrote novelist Kingsley Amis, "that a cold drink should be as cold as possible than that it should be as wet as possible," and tirades: "If he wants fruit salad," said the historian Bernard de Voto of a hapless imbiber contemplating a Bronx, "remind him that cocktails are to be drunk, not eaten."

All cocktails of any age or reputation have their champions, but some have excited more fervor than others. Such is the venerable Mint Julep, pride of the South. Its birthplace is still hotly disputed, with some claiming it for Virginia, some for Kentucky, still others insisting on Georgia. All close ranks, however, when it comes to the sanctity of its preparation: "a sacred rite," said Kentucky's Senator Henry Clay, "that must not be entrusted to a novice, a statistician or a Yankee." Starting with the finest bourbon, this marvel is built up around ice, finely crushed; sugar, extra fine; and mint, fresh, of course.

Within these inviolable limits, there is still margin for interpretation. Regional variations on "authentic" recipes admit crème de menthe, a float of peach brandy or a splash of champagne. Less tolerated is a cavalier approach to the mint. Crushing the defenseless sprig to release the aroma—that ineffable fragrance which permeates the Churchill Downs Clubhouse on Kentucky Derby Day—deeply offends the Virginian sensibility; hence the eloquent deathbed directive of an expiring Virginian, recorded by the novelist Francis Parkinson Keyes: "Never insult a decent woman, never bring in a horse hot to the stable and never crush the mint in a julep."

MINT JULEP

The Mint Julep has been the subject of more ceremony, intense debate and stubborn pride than almost any other cocktail. Should the mint be crushed or not? Should bourbon or rye be used? Should it be served in a tall glass or a silver mug? Should it be garnished with fruit, mint or nothing at all?

What is not controversial is that a tall, sweet Mint Julep is unsurpassed on a warm spring day, when the mint is fresh and the horses are preparing for the Triple Crown.

Muddle four sprigs of mint, one teaspoon of sugar and two teaspoons of water in a tall glass or silver cup. Fill with crushed ice and two ounces of bourbon, and stir. Garnish with fresh mint and a slice of pineapple.

69

The Bloody Mary is another subject of heated controversy. Tomato juice and vodka are uncontestedly the pillars of its reputation, but the secondary ingredients and the method of their integration are as disputed as the origin of the drink. This inspired creation has been attributed with equal authority to Fernand Petiot of Harry's Bar in Paris, who then introduced it to Manhattan in 1934 when he came over to tend bar at the St. Regis, spicing it up with cayenne and Worcestershire Sauce at Prince Serge Obolensky's suggestion; to Felix's Blue Bar in Cannes, where it was originally christened Blood and Guts in honor of General Patton; and to Elsa Maxwell, who, at one of singer Grace Moore's famous Long Island Sunday brunches, was allegedly moved to fortify a "frightfully dull tomato juice" ordered up by a fellow guest.

With its parentage so ambiguous, it is understandable that so many have taken a proprietary role in its confection. The King's Arms Tavern in Williamsburg, Virginia attributes the fame of its Bloody Mary to a homemade horseradish sauce; the Rebels and Redcoats Tavern in Huntington, West Virginia, to fresh lime and celery salt. On the West Coast the enterprising bars have been more creative still in reworking the Bloody Mary to encompass A-1 sauce, cucumbers, celery and green onions —brunch in a glass, drink purists fulminate, waxing positively apoplectic should a wayward aesthetic blend the whole into a frothy gazpacho.

No libation, possibly no art work, has been more eulogized, more hallowed, more hotly debated, than the Martini. It is the most classic of cocktails, to the mixed drink what Rolls Royce is to the automobile, what Baccarat is to crystal. It is so generic

CHAMPAGNE COCKTAIL

Despite its seeming elegance and simplicity, the matter of how, indeed if, a Champagne Cocktail should be made is a matter of impassioned controversy. Those whose awe of the sparkling elixir prevents them from diluting champagne with even a sugar cube are matched in fervor by those who, like Evelyn Waugh, feel that "the excellences of this drink defy description."

Controversy notwithstanding, the Champagne Cocktail is for many the quintessential cocktail, appropriate for any occasion. It is usually made by placing a sugar cube soaked in Angostura bitters in the bottom of a champagne saucer or flute and topping with champagne. Variations incorporate lemon peel, cayenne pepper and a jigger of brandy.

to our image of a cocktail that the three-ounce inverted pyramid on a stem stands as the international symbol for a bar.

Its invention, however, is almost certainly American, and probably bi-coastal. San Francisco attributes its creation to the Occidental Hotel's famed bartender, Jerry Thomas, who is said to have arrived at his inspiration while seeking to slake the thirst of a traveller headed for Martinez. As published in his *Bon Vivant's Companion* of 1862, the Thomas formulation of one part Old Tom Gin to three parts Italian vermouth approaches the sweetness of a candy bar. It is a far cry from the innovation of a barkeep named Martini at New York's Knickerbocker Hotel around 1915 that called for equal parts of London Dry Gin and French vermouth. The holy trinity of gin, vermouth and olives would come later, but the Martini had begun its pilgrimage to the mecca of dryness that would add one part more gin—later vodka—roughly every twenty-five years until today, "dry Martini" has become an alternate way of asking for gin—or vodka—straight up.

Those who fell in with the long march resembled acolytes in an order. It is wondrous that so frail a grail should have called forth so many knights, that so tiny a treat should have engaged so large a portion of thinking men's minds and encouraged them to such excesses of rapture. Conrad Aiken wrote glowingly of the Martini, W. H. Auden composed a haiku to it, and H. L. Mencken, whose wit was generally drier, called it "the only American invention as perfect as a sonnet."

By the thirties the Martini had become a mark of distinction, signaling social ease in the novels of Somerset Maugham and Evelyn Waugh. Even a character from an early Hemingway

novel would say, after downing a couple: "I never tasted anything so cool and lean. They made me feel civilized." Until its transformation in the fifties to the symbol of corporate success, the Martini remained the signature of sophisticates.

Once its status was assured, how to fix a Martini became a matter of some pride and much prejudice, one's recipe as revealing as an old boy's club tie. Cultists became faddish about brands. Somerset Maugham acknowledged only Noilly Prat vermouth; Winston Churchill called out for the gin specially made for The Boodles Club, then, it was said, merely waved the bottle of vermouth over his glass and made an acknowledging bow in the direction of France.

MARTINI

When FDR mixed the first legal cocktail for the cameras to celebrate Repeal, it was no accident that his drink was a Martini. The Martini, with its attendant ceremony replete with wry repartee and a twinkling eye, is part of America's cultural heritage.

A perfect Martini must be served ice cold. Place a tall pitcher or shaker filled with ice in the freezer. Remove the ice when chilled, and add a few fresh cubes to the now-frigid container. Gently stir, or shake, four to ten parts gin with dry vermouth to taste, the quantity generally ranging from one part to a wave of the bottle. Strain into a chilled cocktail glass, and garnish with a twist of lemon peel or an olive on a pick.

Dryness became the matter of ultimate concern. Robert Benchley's solution was "gin and just enough vermouth to take away the nasty, watery look." Ernest Hemingway, on his days off from Papa Dobles, would call out for "Montgomerys." "That's what he called martinis," Harry Cipriani recalls, "because he said that Montgomery liked his odds against the enemy to be fifteen to one and that's how Hemingway wanted the proportion of gin to vermouth."

But none was more vocal than the critic-historian and consummate imbiber Bernard de Voto, who devoted a treatise of some length to "America's supreme gift to the world." "With the martini we reach a fine and noble art," he began, and proceeded to excoriate those transgressors who skimp on ice or incorporate vegetables, reserving his full volley for "the man who mixes his martinis beforehand and keeps them in the refrigerator till cocktail time. You can no more keep a martini in the refrigerator than you can keep a kiss there. The proper union of gin and vermouth is a great and sudden glory; it is one of the happiest marriages on earth and one of the shortest-lived. The fragile tie of ecstasy is broken in a few minutes, and thereafter there can be no remarriage. The beforehander has not understood that what is left, though it was once a martini, can never be one again. He has sinned as seriously as the man who leaves some in a pitcher to drown."

With de Voto's passing, the Martini may have lost its staunchest champion, but its integrity is still being hotly defended. To stir or to shake remains a question, since James Bond reversed the prevailing scripture with his famous

"Shaken, not stirred." In reality the only difference is aesthetic, in that stirring a Martini leaves it clear, while shaking renders it cloudy. Nevertheless, the choice of technique is a matter of pride to the finer establishments. New York's Colony Club shakes, the neighboring St. Regis stirs; San Francisco's Plaza Hotel shakes, the Stanford Court stirs; and so it goes.

Concerning the lemon peel: Mauro Lotti, barlord of Rome's Grand Hotel, insists first on washing it, then twisting it to float the oils, then discarding it. Dennis, at London's Claridge's, drops the peel in. Kevin Kaeff, bar manager of the Hotel Bel Air in Los Angeles, rubs the rim with one peel, discards it and slips in a fresh one for the look.

Concerning the olive: "Happiness," said Johnny Carson, "is a hungry man finding two olives in his martini." Certainly, an unpitted pair skewered diagonally along the side of the glass is the most classic presentation, but there are many who hold that a single olive placed ceremoniously at the bottom is more refined. All agree, however, that only the very small ones are tolerable, in that they displace the least liquid, and preferably those of a particular green: "Only seventeen or so out of a can of a hundred are fit to make the perfect martini," insisted Matt Kane of Matt Kane's in Washington, D. C.

The gospels read on. Only glass shakers, say those who suspect that even chrome imparts a taste. Only metal shakers, say the devotees of chill. In warmer climes the search for absolute zero has led to such extremes of perfection as those still practiced at Tony's in Houston, which keeps its martini glasses and four brands of gin in the freezer.

So might the Martini have ossified into an artifact, but for the vagaries of fashion and the national predilection to experiment. The initial storming of the barricade substituted a pearl onion for the olive, creating the Gibson. There followed the lapse of the Dillatini, in which the garnish is a dilly bean; the Rosalind Russell, which replaces gin with aquavit; the Sakitini; the Tequini; and, most recently, the spicy Cajun Martini. However, the only serious contender is the Vodkatini, which currently outsells its forebear three to one. No one has stepped forward to claim it, but every drinker from the fifties can name a bartender who insists he invented the Vodka Martini.

⚊Y⚊

Men behind bars—they are there to greet you, to remember your name, to keep you company across the mahogany. But first and foremost, bartenders are there to mix drinks. In the alchemy of the cocktail, the bartender is Merlin, conjuring magical libations from the line-up of spirits, flavored waters and garnishes that surround him. He performs in the open, so his technique must be flawless. Under close scrutiny of the critical and the expectant, a bartender practicing his art must be prepared to shake, squeeze, swizzle, stir, swirl, strain, frost, blend and garnish.

He must be creative. In one day, recalled Oscar, long-time wizard of the Waldorf, he might be asked for something "sweet, dry, peppery, fruity, refreshing, smooth, vigorous, velvety, tangy or rich."

His performance must have range: "the virtuosity," Francois Mouvet, a thirty-year veteran of Scandia in Los Angeles, puts

MANHATTAN

Invented in 1880 and named for the Manhattan Club, rather than the island, Manhattans come sweet or dry, depending on whether sweet Italian or dry French vermouth is used. In most bars, the sweet variety is served unless dry is requested.

The usual proportion for a Manhattan is two parts bourbon to one part vermouth, adding a dash of Angostura. Shake the ingredients with ice, and strain into a cocktail glass. Garnish with a maraschino cherry.

BLUE HAWAIIAN

Lesser known than other warm-weather coolers such as the Piña Colada or the Margarita, the Blue Hawaiian is equally refreshing, its blue color belying a pineapple, coconut and orange flavor.

Blend a measure of light rum, a half-measure of blue Curaçao, two measures of pineapple juice and a measure of cream of coconut with crushed ice. Serve with a short straw in a goblet or old-fashioned glass. Garnish with a pineapple slice.

it, "to rim one goblet with salt, rub another with mint, while properly building up a Pousse Cafe"; and finesse: "It takes years," says the legendary Bertin, who practiced his magic at the Ritz in Paris, "to learn how to slip a lemon peel into a three ounce martini without displacing anything liquid."

What is more, all this artistry must be practiced at sleight-of-hand speed. On busy nights orders fly in like darts; one Tom Collins, two Sazeracs, one Singapore Sling, one Sea Breeze—load the ice. He who hesitates is lost, for the cocktail has but one shining, golden moment before it begins to dissolve.

Since a top barkeep prides himself on never reaching for the wrong bottle, he must have the memory of a computer to handle all the possible combinations. The roster of cocktails is enormous—at one time Harry's New York Bar offered over eight hundred—and a bartender of the old school wouldn't be caught dead looking up the ingredients of any of them. In the fecund days of the twenties, when the repertoire of fizzes, cobblers, slings and rickeys was longer than a Penn Station timetable, with new cocktails being invented every day, it was a matter of pride for a San Francisco barkeep to field some smart aleck New Yorker's request for a Lizard Skin with "Coming right up!"

In the short term, of course, the customer is always right. Chivas and Cola? You got it. Still, there is always a point at which a true professional draws the line. When master-caterer John Childs was tending bar in Seattle, he once responded to a request for a "very, very dry martini" with an empty glass. When Waring introduced the blender, opening up the world

to slushes, the bartenders of New York's crusty Algonquin Hotel banded together in their refusal to use one.

Roger Gillmore, who tended the bar at Chez Jay in Venice, California in the sixties, when the artists used to hang out there, is still remembered for the evening when a Texan strolled in, plunked a fistful of twenties on the counter and asked for "somethin' U-nique." Gillmore deftly scooped up the money, stuffed it in the blender along with crème de menthe and crushed ice, then poured it into a martini glass. "You got it," he said as he presented the rich blend, "a U. S. Mint frappe. That'll be three dollars, please."

The request for a new drink is, of course, the bartender's big chance. The success of his response might constitute a new page in the history of the cocktail, and with it his immortality.

The twenties were the bonanza time in the prospecting for new cocktails, producing nuggets like the Bridal, the Adonis, the Passion and the Gloom Lifter. Some, like the Bunny Hug, reflected dance fads of the day; others, like the Strike-Off, more serious concerns. Provocative names dropped hints of wild promise: Bosom Caresser, Maiden's Blush, Between the Sheets, Widow's Kiss.

Stars courting publicity showed up nightly at bars, and barkeeps returned the favor by creating drinks in their names. Mary Pickford had a cocktail named for her; Douglas Fairbanks, two. The Fay Wray combined champagne and peach brandy; the Marlene Dietrich, Cherry Heering liqueur on ice with vodka and a cherry; the John Wayne, Jack Daniels on ice with a dash of Pernod. For Cary Grant, when he switched from gin on the rocks to vodka and water, Bru Mysak of the "21" Club put to-

WHISKEY SOUR

Sours, which combine citrus juice, sugar and spirits, were first popularized in the 1850s, with the Whiskey Sour dating from 1891. Proportions may vary according to taste, but the standard formula is one part sweet, two parts sour and eight parts strong, usually bourbon or Canadian whisky.

Shake sugar syrup, lemon juice and whiskey with ice, and strain into a sour glass. When the sugar syrup is omitted, the drink is called a Palmer.

85

gether two ounces of Absolut, a dash of Tio Pepe and a tinge of Rose's lime juice, which then went on the menu as the Cary Grant Cocktail.

When cocktail mania subsided in the fifties and sixties, the old-timers went back to the basics of their trade, content to curate the classics and to build a reputation on who made them best.

"One thing I've never had sent back is a martini," says Gus Tassopulos, who tended the bar at the Beverly Hills Hotel for twenty-five years. "They come in here from San Francisco and tell me that my Irish Coffee is the best in the West," says Art Doyle, a veteran barkeep of Bergin's in Los Angeles. And at the Oak Bar in New York they are still lining up to watch Mose Perracchio incarnate his infallible Whiskey Sour.

Amateurs can only hope to rival the technique of these professional ministers to the parched. Building up a Separator, for example, so that no spiritous layer importunes another, is surely beyond reach. So, undoubtedly, is the "twiddle," that supreme art of the mixing process that calls for placing the thumb lightly on top of a long spoon, then twirling the fingers to revolve the spoon at an incredible speed.

IRISH COFFEE

Coffee has served as everything from an antiseptic to a source of poetic inspiration, so its inclusion in a cocktail was only a matter of time. The Italians did it with Galliano and Amaretto, the Danes with Aquavit. But coffee's finest expression may be the Irish Coffee.

Combine a large shot of Irish Whiskey and hot coffee in a mug. Sugar to taste, and top with a dollop of whipped cream.

ROB ROY

The Rob Roy, made with scotch and sweet red vermouth, takes its name from Robert MacGregor, Scotland's Robin Hood and a legendary redhead, Roy being the Scottish nickname for a man with red hair. Also known as a Scotch Manhattan, the Rob Roy has a smoky flavor due to the substitution of scotch for bourbon.

Combine two or three parts scotch with one part sweet vermouth and a dash of Angostura bitters. Garnish with a cherry. Variations include the substitution of orange bitters for Angostura, creating a Highland Fling, and the addition of a dash of Drambuie, making a Bobbie Burns.

It might be argued that the Martini cult went a little too far, but no serious mixologist will dispute that the creation of a cocktail has its ground rules, and that mixing drinks requires the mastery of some basic principles.

1. First and foremost, use plenty of ice. Cocktails must be served arctic cold. The exceptions are toddies and Irish Coffee, which should be served equator hot.

2. Add liquor to ice cubes, not vice versa.

3. Always serve quality spirits.

4. Use fresh juice, unless otherwise specified, and crisp vegetables for garnish.

5. To prepare peels for garnish or a twist, first wash them, then remove the bitter pith.

6. Soak orange and lemon slices in warm water to extract more juice, then cover with a damp cloth to prevent their drying out. Avoid slicing so finely that they curl and droop.

7. Use only super-fine sugar so that it dissolves completely.

8. Stir cocktails that require mixing only twice; those that call for stirring, a minimum of seven times. Cocktails prepared in shakers may not be rocked side to side. Shake them in a vigorous up-and-down motion, up to twelve times for a fizz.

9. Always strain before serving, taking care to remove the ice from the shaker so as not to dilute the second serving.

10. Chill glasses beforehand, and present all cocktails in the appropriate glassware.

BLITHE IMBIBERS

"They found that the fountain of youth
Was a mixture of gin and vermouth."
—Cole Porter, "Two Little Babes in the Wood"

They moved with the seasons, boarding yachts in Palm Beach and trains in Madrid. They flocked to St. Moritz for the snow, to Aix-Les-Bains for the waters and to Paris for the experience. They bathed naked in the Aegean and splashed fully dressed in the fountains of Rome. They worked on Wall Street and played at the Waldorf, became engaged in the Rainbow Room and divorced in Nevada. They smoked, they boogied, they partied and they drank cocktails—cold, mixed, marvellous cocktails.

As a species, the cocktail people emerged in the twenties, a tribe of ardent spirits with a predisposition to the cup that cheers. They radiated good times and good humor according to a gospel adapted from Ecclesiastes, that man hath no better thing than to eat well and drink heartily that he may be merry.

Their *modus bibendi* was to become fluent in the changing vocabulary of pick-me-ups, to bring back exotic drink recipes from faraway places, to proceed nightly from party to restaurant to clubs that never closed. They retained supreme confidence in the magic of the libation, in the conviction that should the world go on the rocks, a little top up with good spirits would float it to safety.

Albeit upstarts of our century, this bibulous tribe descended from old and noble lineage. They could lay claim to Cleopatra, who had a reputation for dissolving pearls in her wine; to that eager epicurean Petronius, whose call to the banquet was "Let's wet our whistles!"; and to his feckless master, Nero, who tippled while Rome burned.

GIMLET

A descendant of Admiral Edward Vernon's scurvy-preventing rum and lime juice combinations, the Gimlet was the mainstay of the British in many a torrid and inhospitable corner of the far-flung empire.

Made with either gin or vodka, the Gimlet is currently mixed in London's Savoy Bar in the simple ratio of three parts spirits to one part Rose's lime juice. Mix the ingredients with ice in a mixing glass, then strain the contents into a cocktail glass.

From the Middle Ages they could point to Chaucer, who sent his merry band along his own well-travelled route to the inns of Canterbury: "So was their jolly whistle well y-wet." And from the Renaissance, there were those splendid quaffers the Medici, and the impressionable Cervantes, who expressed his readiness gracefully: "I drink when I have occasion and sometimes when I have no occasion."

The satirist Samuel Butler advocated asylums for teetotalers. Lord Byron applied meter to his lines of least resistance: "Let's have wine and women, mirth and laughter/soda and water the day after." Champagne was Napoleon's talisman; he partook of it unfailingly before every major battle, except, to his misfortune, before Waterloo. That other great martial statesman of the nineteenth century, Count Otto von Bismarck, had like priorities; when his Prussian armies occupied France, he ordered the troops to spare her greatest treasure: "Gentlemen, patriotism stops at Champagne!"

In the pantheon of the spirited, a place of honor must be reserved for those men of bounty and flair like the Earl of Coventry, who gave away port by the caseful; the Prince de Conti, who ordered three bottles of Madeira consecrated to the sauce of one ham; and the convivial Charles Dickens, whose penchant as a young man for inviting friends in for "Scotch whisky and cigars" launched a lifelong reputation for the capacity and quality of his cellar and the generosity of his table. There was no rum quencher or whisky toddy or champagne punch contributing to the comfort of the Pickwickians that Dickens hadn't personally concocted. "There are strings in the human heart which must never be sounded by another, and

drinks that I make myself are those strings in mine," he once wrote. Upon falling ill, England's irrational treasure balked at a directive that he abstain from porter, an English malt ale. "I done it though," he later boasted, but only by switching to gin.

The most direct line of American descent was via the Founding Fathers, whose enshrinement of alcohol in the order of things was, if not constitutional, certainly sainted. "Reflect," urged Benjamin Franklin, "on the position God has given the elbow. By its present location, we see it designed so that we can drink at our ease, with the glass coming just to the mouth. Let us then adore, glass in hand, that wise benevolence; let us adore and drink."

In the century to follow, his advice was well taken, not least of all by Capitol Hill. Henry Clay first introduced Mint Juleps to Washington, and Daniel Webster proposed, at a typically well-supplied dinner, his famous resolution to the national debt: "Yes, gentlemen," he cried, taking out his wallet, "it should be paid, and I'll be hanged if it shan't be. I'll pay it myself. How much is it?" Hawkers sold liquor from the Capitol's crypt, and the doorkeeper, when seeking the senators for a roll call, knew to find them in the restaurants one floor below, where deceivingly strong water was dispensed from pitchers and teapots. "Pale sherry" was the password for undiluted gin; "brown sherry" obtained brandy. Well into the present century, the member who requested cold tea with a wink in a House or Senate restaurant was served whiskey in his teacup.

Even the abstemious Lincoln, who had operated a tavern prior to entering politics, championed spirits. "The making of liquor," he said, "is regarded as an honorable livelihood. If people are injured from the use of liquor, the injury arises not from the use of a bad thing but from the abuse of a good thing." When challenged by prohibitionists, he justified his position in an address to the Washingtonian Society. "When all such of us as have now reached the years of maturity first opened our eyes upon the stage of existence, we found intoxicating liquor recognized by everybody, repudiated by nobody. It commonly entered into the first draught of the infant and the last of the dying man."

The gender reference was significant. Women, it must be noted, were given no stake in the world of liquor straight up. Their place was strictly in the home, sipping syllabubs and cordials. Even when social custom relaxed enough to allow wives to dine in public with their husbands, women still might drink only wine with propriety. As late as the turn of the century, a young lady of standing, assigned three chaperones and no fun, never tasted a cocktail until after she was married.

It fell to the avant-garde, women decked in the war paint of face powder and rouge, to expand their indecorous thirst for the knowledge of all things to the liquid encyclopedia of spiritous beverages. After having crossed the Rubicon of the Martini and the Manhattan, the more militant among them arranged to be photographed sipping Whiskey Sours in the sanctuary of the Oak Room of the Plaza Hotel, thus securing for themselves, a good decade before the vote, their inalienable right to the cocktail.

With women squarely aboard, the young century sailed into a new age of drinking, when a cocktail was as much a part of what the world had to offer as a stylish new hat or a shiny red

TOP BANANA

No second banana this, the Top Banana is a special warm weather pleasure which combines the tangy boost of fresh oranges with the subtle, smoothness of bananas.

Pour a shot of vodka, a shot of crème de banana and the juice of half an orange into a cocktail shaker. Shake with cracked ice, and strain into an old-fashioned glass.

bicycle; a time when the young and the idle, in tune with their age, saw life itself as a cocktail, half gin and half jazz, and their elders, albeit to the slower moving fox-trot, danced right along with them.

The profile of the modern imbiber highlights every facet of the human personality. One thinks of urbanity, people who knew the world and how to deal with it: the cool elegance of George Sanders as The Saint, offering Brandy and Sodas; the aplomb of Cary Grant, a Martini in his hand and Katharine Hepburn on his lap.

One thinks of flirtation: Mae West as Flower Belle Lee, slipping out of her Whiskey and Water with "I generally avoid temptation unless I can't resist it."

One thinks of resilience: Winston Churchill's well-supported claim that "I have taken more out of alcohol than alcohol has taken out of me."

One thinks of flamboyance: the glass of Chivas Regal Nathan Milstein places on the fragile veneer of his Stradivarius when demonstrating his flair with a rousing Sousa march.

A penchant for enjoyment, perhaps, but never for excess, cocktail people didn't booze, or guzzle, or tope. Liquor, observed O. Henry, always rubbed them the right way. Modern imbibers drank to a new rhythm. They drank socially; they drank faddishly; they drank for fun. They had *savoir boire.* As Diana Vreeland puts it: "People were still drinking, it's just that suddenly everyone was mixing Martinis. And what's more," she recalls, "they were so entertaining."

And never were they wittier than when commenting on their preferred form of pleasure. Will Sinclair, a prominent figure of Fisher Island in its heyday, was cherished for his retort to the ridiculous query as to whether he would care for a drink: "The only time I ever said no to that was when I misunderstood the question." There was Robert Benchley's classic one-liner; "Get me out of this wet suit and into a dry martini." There was Sir Winston's priceless rejoinder to Lady Astor's outraged "Sir, you are drunk!" "And you, Madam, are ugly. The difference is that tomorrow I will be sober." And there is the entire repertoire of W. C. Fields, whose contributions to the *biblica alcoholica* are immortal.

Bartender to Fields as he serves his Martini: "Would you like a lemon peel?"

Fields: "If I wanted a lemonade I would ask for it."

Maitre d' of Hollywood's Brown Derby, on a day Fields had a hangover: "Alka Seltzer, perhaps?"

Fields: "Alka Seltzer? Damn it, the noise of it would kill me!"

The day that a stagehand foolishly topped up the thespian's mason jars that were euphemistically marked "grapefruit juice" with the real thing, Fields shot off his celebrated jeremiad: "Who put grapefruit juice in my grapefruit juice?" And finally on his muse: "I remember well the woman who first led me to drink; I'm going to write and thank her for it."

SIDECAR
Invented in Paris during World War I, some say at Harry's New York Bar, this cocktail was named for the motorcycle sidecar in which its inventor was transported to and from the bistros and cafes. The Sidecar has undergone a tremendous simplification process since its conception, and what was originally concocted using some seven or eight ingredients has now become equal parts brandy, triple sec and lemon juice. When served as an aperitif, the proportion of brandy is often raised and that of triple sec lowered.

As diverse as snowflakes, if equally prone to liquidity, the great imbibers of our century have approached their favorite pastime from all points on the palate. There have been the sensualists, those seekers of heady aroma who knew how to send potent potables eighty ways around the tongue. "Everything starts in the mouth," said Salvador Dali, who asked of any fine distillation that it "linger awhile in the heady orifice to be carried to every membrane of memory and dream." Thus stemmed Somerset Maugham's position in the Martini debate: "They should always be stirred not shaken so that the molecules lie sensuously on top of each other."

There were the ritualists, spiritual descendents of Henry Clay, that enlightened Senator from Kentucky who insisted one "maintain a deep reverence for the ingredients and a proper appreciation of the occasion." One thinks of Bernard de Voto whose cult of the Martini ran to fanaticism, of Ian Fleming who prepared his rum punch as if it were a rite. Cole Porter, too, was known to be particular about all form relating to cocktails. Precisely two were served before dinner parties, and woe to the hapless who transgressed. One poor fellow who did was never invited again; "He simply won't do," was the way Cole had put it, "and besides, he wore brown shoes."

For such gourmets of the liquor table, ceremony is all, and brand discrimination is critical. There can be no such thing as "just making do." To make himself a sangria, Vincent Astor once summoned to his table at "21" a bottle of Romanée Conti '47, a bottle of Dom Pérignon, Cognac, Curaçao and fresh fruit. In the event of separation from a reliable supply source, the cherished libation must be secured on one's person. Well after Repeal, Tiffany and Company did brisk business in mono-grammed silver flasks. Joan Crawford used to carry her own supply of vodka around with her. "She would request two glasses with ice," recalled Hollywood columnist George Christy of an evening he joined her for dinner, "fill them up herself and ask the waiter to add two vodkas to her bill."

Even in the haven of an established bar, the ritualists can be formal about mixing their own. Lady Sylvia Ashley, a noted figure of Hollywood's glamour days, was reputed to be totally helpless in the ways of the world, except at the cocktail hour, when she would smile sweetly at the bartender of Chasen's and ask permission to fix her own Bloody Marys. In more recent times, when Sears Roebuck heir Edgar Stern travels to bars where he can't mix his own Martinis, he hands the barman a card with detailed directives.

Less particular is his uncle, David Stern, who tosses out an order for a Martini and waits to see what arrives. Once, when asked to specify what kind of Martini, he answered, "Oh, just the old fashioned kind" and was served a standard Martini with all the ingredients of an Old Fashioned, minus the whiskey, and partook of it pleasurably. His is a catholicism of taste Heywood Broun would have admired; "Any port in a storm," Broun once said of an inferior liquor.

Chief exponent of the *laisser-boire* school of drinking was H. L. Mencken, Baltimore's eminent man of letters, who proved himself friendly to all spirituous beverages, inimical to none. "I am ombibulous: I drink every known drink and enjoy them all." In support of this claim Mencken once had a mathematician tabulate the number of possible cocktail combinations; the

BLACK RUSSIAN

Simple and elegant, the Black Russian is one of America's most popular cocktails and also one of the few not invented in the United States. The Black Russian came to life behind the bar of the Hôtel Metropole in Brussels.

Combine a shot of vodka and a shot of coffee-flavoured liqueur, such as Kahlua or Tia Maria, over ice in a rocks glass. To make a White Russian, top with a float of cream.

figure arrived at was 17,864,392,788. Mencken claimed to have mixed up 273 of them at random and found them all to his liking.

Subscribers to Mencken's all-encompassing tastes had to keep all options open. Colorado tycoon Spencer Penrose made this plain when asked why he maintained a costly membership in the exclusive Pacific Union Club when he hadn't visited San Francisco in over a decade. "My God, man," he exclaimed, "I might want a drink out there!"

They had to be brilliantly resourceful in winkling oases out of deserts. Kingsley Amis devised a failsafe technique: "With a bottle of Angostura you can make a drink anywhere." Once, when Averell Harriman, then Ambassador to Great Britain, motored down to Charters to dine with Winston Churchill, he found the warlord on his knees before the sideboard vainly seeking vermouth to wave over his Martini. Frustration lasted but the moment it took to decide that the remedy might be a drop of Madeira, whereupon the Martinis were forgotten as they set to work on the bottle of Madeira. Harriman recalled it for his godson Peter Duchin as an "exceptional" evening, though the dinner, presumably, was entirely irrelevant.

That food for Churchill generally remained marginal to the liquid business at hand was made a matter of record on the occasion of a banquet of London barristers held in his honor. When inquiry was made as to what fare would best please their illustrious guest, the reply came back: "He doesn't mind what food you serve as long as it is prefaced with a martini. Serve champagne with the meal, brandy afterwards. And if the party lasts late, serve whisky and soda for the nightcap."

Members of this dedicated school of drinking could be counted on, in the ultimate emergency, to bring spirits to the rescue, a technique perfected on boats and the various vehicles pertaining to air. Thus did Prince Serge Obolensky, that master of all ceremonies, once save a rocky cruise on Vincent Astor's yacht *Nourmahal*; when asked by his host how best to allay the panic of his passengers, the Prince calmly called for a bottle of vodka. And it is well documented that David Niven, fearful of heights, would only go up in his Jules Verne balloon for *Around the World in 80 Days* after Mike Todd supplied him with a survival kit of champagne.

Needless to say, for Mencken and his kind teetotalers were a breed apart. "A man who has taken aboard two or three cocktails is less competent than he was before to steer a battleship down the Ambrose Channel, or to cut off a leg, or to draw up a deed of trust, or to conduct Bach's B minor mass, but he is immensely more competent to entertain a dinner party, or to admire a pretty girl, or to hear Bach's B minor mass. The harsh, useful things of the world, from pulling teeth to digging potatoes, are best done by men who are as starkly sober as so many convicts in the death-house, but the lovely useless things, the charming and exhilarating things, are best done by men with, as the phrase is, a few sheets in the wind. Pithecanthropus erectus was a teetotaler, but the angels, you may be sure, know what is proper at 5 p.m."

A temporary sojourn into the netherworld of abstinence was permitted for a lucrative bet or a lapse into fitness, as long as in the short run one came to one's senses. There had been fears for the humorist Don Marquis, who had misguidedly gone on the wagon until happily, one month and one day after this errant decision, he walked up to the bar of the Players Club and announced, "I've conquered my god damn will power." The point, as the enthusiasts saw it, was that abstinence was sad for you, a certainty that Robert Mitchum once tried to convey to an audience he was addressing. "There are, I believe, some of you who never touch alcohol in any shape or form. I respect your convictions wholeheartedly, but I am sincerely sorry for you at the same time. For when you wake up in the morning that's as good as you're ever gonna feel."

No corner of the nation lacked its contingent of notable drinkers. For three glamorous decades the Hollywood cocktail colony comprised virtually every star in the firmament. The "It" girl Clara Bow slaked her craving for exotic refreshments with a nightery of her own, the "It" Club, which launched a new cocktail every week. Will Rogers quenched his thirst after polo matches so regularly at the bar of the Beverly Hills Hotel that they named it the Polo Lounge.

Douglas Fairbanks set up a private saloon at United Artists with a twenty-foot table so laden with bottles that fishing rods were provided to reel in the label of one's choice. Jean Harlow liked to shimmy on dance floors holding blue cocktails. Greta Garbo was wedded to her vodka, though she would never live down her first spoken screen words: "Give me a whiskey, with ginger ale on the side—and don't be stingy." When seated between a brace of swank gentlemen, Norma Shearer would hold a Martini in each hand so that whether speaking to the right or the left, she could flirt over the rim of her glass. Newcomer Marilyn Monroe showed a fancy for Bullshots without knowing what was in them. "That's bouillon and vodka, Marilyn," her date explained. "Bouillon?" she breathed, "What a terrible thing to do to vodka!"

On the theory that the world was three drinks behind, Humphrey Bogart founded the celebrated Holmby Hills Rat Pack, originally a drinking club with by-laws and meetings, whose members included such of the glamorous parched as Frank Sinatra, David Niven, Spencer Tracy and Irving "Swifty" Lazar. The club eventually consolidated around Sinatra and his Clan: Sammy Davis, Jr., Dean Martin, Peter Lawford and Jack

SAZERAC
Popularized at the bar of New Orleans's Hotel Roosevelt in the early 20th century, the Sazerac actually dates back to 1820, deriving its name from the confections of Antoine Peychaud, the New Orleans apothecary whose "coquetiers," the predecessers of American cocktails, were made with Sazerac du Forge brandy. At one time, as was the case with many early cocktails, the word "sazerac" was Southern for mixed drink.

A dry and pungent cocktail, today's Sazerac is essentially an Old Fashioned made with Peychaud bitters and flavored with a dash of Pernod (absinthe without the illegal wormwood). In a mixing glass, combine a teaspoon of sugar, three dashes of Peychaud bitters and two shots of Bourbon, and stir with large ice cubes. Rinse the inside of a chilled old-fashioned glass with Pernod, then strain in the drink. Garnish with a twisted lemon peel. The Sazerac is often served with a glass of ice water as a chaser.

Daniels, the latter so indispensable that when Sinatra went to Monaco to sing for the Royals, he brought along twelve cases lest the Hôtel de Paris be deficient in Tennessee Sour Mash.

While Hollywood had its movie stars, New York had its theater crowd, which kept the bars of 42nd Street hopping hours after the last curtain fell. Broadway luminaries such as John Barrymore, Helen Hayes, the Alfred Lunts and Shirley Booth created the standing ovation tradition at Sardi's, appearing at midnight to toasts and applause.

Lunchtime drinking was preempted by the writers, who gathered around tables at the Algonquin and the Puncheon Club, sharpening their wits on Martinis and their pencils, when copy was due, on more-forgiving Orange Blossoms. Some years later the southern contingent, William Faulkner, Terry Southern and Tennessee Williams wrote in on the serious spirits. "Wine," Williams had said, paraphrasing Dr. Johnson, "is for women, whiskey for men, but brandy is for heroes."

In Washington, a fondness for alcohol blended with politics like gin with vermouth, and even the Eighteenth Amendment failed to deter its architects. FDR proudly mixed "the first legal martini" after Repeal in the Oval Office before a host of news cameras. Although under his administration more than one round was rarely served before dinner, it was well known that if you desired another, you had only to follow Harry Hopkins upstairs to the private supply.

When the liquor ran dry at home, the more impatient or the wealthier or the less employed pursued wetter climates abroad. They trailed Hemingway to Spain for the bullfights and Fundador. They joined John Dos Passos on the Riviera for brandy

and gambling. They followed the painter and writer Ludwig Bemelmans to St. Moritz for the novel fizz drinks Gustav was creating at the bar of the Palace Hotel; Louis Bromfield found them irresistible to the point of several returns, while Erich Maria Remarque, who had started literary life as a columnist on cocktails, moved right in, establishing Gustav's bar as the base from which he would write *Arc de Triomphe*.

Yet another contingent went to London, to carouse with the "dukerati," as the poet William Sansom tagged the literary people and the titled who toasted daybreak at David Tennant's Gargoyle, and to hobnob with Bohemia at the Cafe Royal, where Oscar Wilde had held court with kir at lunchtime and

KIR ROYALE

The very popular Kir Royale is a sweet and sparkling wine aperitif which take its color and flavor from cassis, a French liqueur made from black currant berries.

In a champagne flute, combine champagne with half a shot of cassis. A Kir Royale is unequalled as a cocktail with which to toast a special moment, but it is also appropriate before and with a meal.

where the Bloomsbury group gathered after hours to gossip over Veuve Cliquot Rose.

Eventually, when they had nibbled at all Europe and found it to their taste, this exuberant flock settled in Paris, where the living was easy, dazzling and cheap. At twilight they convened in the cafes of Montparnasse, where pretenders to the Great American Novel and journalists trailing gossip had been piling up saucers since noon. "The world is a large, large oyster, but I do not think I will choke when I swallow it," penned Thomas Wolfe from the Dôme, while over at the Procope e. e. cummings ordered Scotch and Water. "So this is Paris," he wrote, "i will sit in the corner and drink thinks and think drinks…waiter a drink waiter two or three drinks."

The writers' tastes were the most fully recorded, but in the experience of Jimmy Charters—a barman so popular in the Paris of the twenties that his fans followed him from one bar to the other—the painters and photographers surpassed them, going for Mandarine, Amer Picon and Pernod "in a large way." They generally had to back off though. "At the end of a month most of them switch to something milder, usually cocktails, fizzes, or other fancy drinks," and Jimmy was standing right by with one of his fancier libations. One in particular, a daring innovation that combined Cognac, Mandarine, Amer Picon, Pernod, and cherry brandy, seduced even the French, as biographer Laurence Vail would remind him: "Many times I have known Antheil and Varese, Kisling, Derain and Van Dongen to seek inspiration and exhilaration in your artful long drinks."

114

And so, increasingly, did the women, those daughters and wives of the day's rich and famous, who traded in their allowances for bobbed hair and one-way tickets across the Atlantic: willful Nathalie Bryher, carefree Flossie Martin, careless Zelda Fitzgerald, and, close on their heels, their eccentric English counterparts, stylish Iris Tree, literary Mary Beerbohm and the impetuous Nancy Cunard. Cut loose from their motherlands, intellectuals, heiresses and waifs cast anchor together in bars, cafes and clubs, creating a climate in which the expression of all ideas was permissable.

All who later recorded the expatriate years recalled them as a brilliant fireworks of creativity and confusion tossed up together like the very cocktails that inspired them. Hart Crane condensed it all on a postcard to a friend. "Dinners, soirees, poets, erratic millionaires, painters, translations, lobsters, absinthe, music, promenades, oysters, sherry, aspirins, pictures, Sapphic heiresses, editors, books, sailors. And how!"

Then suddenly it was over. The wherewithal had run out: the salary, the stipend and those precious checks from home, cut off by the Depression and the rumblings of war. With no one left to drink with and no more credit at the bars, the message was clear: go on the wagon or go home.

Ironically, the once trend-setting expatriates were as out of synch with the local drinking scene to which they returned as they were with the somber Europe they had left behind. A Scotch-on-the-Rocks contingent spun off with Dashiell Hammett to the livelier entertainments of Harlem's nightclubs uptown, and some old companions still hung around to trade stories along the mahogany, soon to be joined by working

SLOE GIN FIZZ

Deep red, bubbly and sweet, the Sloe Gin Fizz takes its name and derives its color from Sloe Gin, a liqueur made of London Dry Gin steeped in sloe or blackthorn berries to give it their unique flavor.

Observing the standard proportions for a fizz, use roughly one part citrus juice, two parts sugar syrup, three parts sloe gin and four parts soda water. Combine the first three ingredients with ice in a shaker. Shake vigorously, and pour into a chilled fizz glass. While stirring, top with soda water.

GRASSHOPPER

Mingling the flavors of mint and chocolate, the Grasshopper is a perfect end to an elegant meal, a sophisticated dessert in itself.

In a shaker with cracked ice, combine equal parts of white crème de cacao, green crème de menthe and cream. Serve in a cocktail glass or champagne saucer. Garnish with shaved chocolate.

women without men at their sides. But the war the returning Americans had sought to avoid followed them home, spelling an end to the heady days of frolic and fun and leading the cocktail into more sedate and settled surroundings

A short decade later the Martini decamped to corporate headquarters as the mixed drink was appropriated by the expense account crowd of executives, agents and television personalities who were carving out a climate where the newest cocktail on the circuit was the very dry Dow Jones. Nostalgia for the glory days waned in the following decades as the nation focussed its attention on the more compelling priorities of self-awareness in the sixties and health in the seventies, seeking immortality through a new regimen of early to rise and early to bed and prodigal diets of alfalfa and carrot juice.

H. L. Mencken would have railed at such extremist behavior, dismissing its assumptions as suspect, if not slanderous. Were not spirits the condition of life everlasting? Rabelais himself had ordained it; "Always drink and you'll never die." And in the event of a fatal misunderstanding, the real trouper was expected to toast the final hours in the spirit of the occasion. He could follow the example set by Count Taittinger, who explained his dying request for a tumbler of water to his children as merely "because one must before death be reconciled with one's enemies."

RAMOS FIZZ

The brothers Ramos thrived in the French Quarter in 19th-century New Orleans. Of this drink, history records that a phalanx of eight to twelve liveried waiters at the Ramos' Imperial Saloon passed the cocktail shaker over their shoulders, one to the other, shaking, chilling and frothing the drink. Today the fresh, light Ramos Fizz is frequently enjoyed as a mid-morning cocktail.

In a shaker, combine two jiggers of gin, an egg white, a jigger of cream, three dashes of orange flower water and the juice of half a lemon. Shake vigorously, strain into a fizz glass or goblet, and add a dash of soda water.

THE HOME OF THE COCKTAIL

"Meet me at the Numerical Place at the rich man's dawn

and we will have our psyches half-soled."

(Translation: "Meet me at the '21' at 6:00 P. M.

and we'll have a drink.")

—Eddie Condon

One hundred million highballs ago, when this land was young and water was too dangerous to drink, America's forefathers sought out quarters where they might quaff the safer liquids and, while they were about it, air their grievances, plot their uprisings and deal with the general business of revolution.

What better place to brace their resolution and fortify their union than a snug and cheerful "ordinary" resembling those already common in the countries from which they had so recently migrated. The colonists dreamed longingly of the *auberge*, the *gasthaus* and, most nostalgically, of the tavern, an establishment dating back to thirteenth-century London, whence it evolved into those roisterous places of good fellowship that were to provide so close a model for the first home of the cocktail.

Their names were delicious corruptions like Bag O'Nails, for "bacchanalia," and Elephant and Castle, for Isabelle of Castille. At one time Fleet Street numbered as many taverns as dwellings. Among the more prominent establishments were The Devil and St. Dunstan, popular since the days of James I, when the playwright Ben Jonson presided over the congenial Apollo Club, and later favored by the fashionable highwayman Mull "Sack" Cottington, so nicknamed for his predilection for spiced sherry; The Crown, whose hapless landlord, overheard to say his son "would inherit The Crown," was executed for treason by Edward IV; The Goose and The Gridiron, rendezvous of the Freemasons when Christopher Wren was Grandmaster; and The Mermaid,

frequented by Shakespeare and Sir Walter Raleigh, of which Keats would write: "Souls of poets dead and gone/What Elysium have ye known/ Happy field or merry cavern/Cheerier than the Mermaid Tavern."

London offered inns for every inclination. For the romantics there was The Gun, where Lord Nelson trysted with Lady Hamilton. The Bull and Bush was where Charles II stopped in for a top-up and was offered an orange by a comely lass, which he accepted on the condition that she peel it at the palace; no problem, smiled Nell Gwynne, as she raced upstairs for her hat.

For carousing there was Ye Olde Cock Tavern where Samuel Pepys took the noted actress Mrs. Knip "and drank, eat a lobster, and sang, and mighty merry." At The Boar's Head, where Falstaff had years before debauched, one James Austin, inventor, invited his cronies to partake of a brandy pudding that weighed two thousand pounds; it had boiled for two weeks at the Red Lion Inn and was being paraded over to the accompaniment of a band, when a gaggle of Londoners routed the escort and gobbled the mighty dessert before the Austin contingent had as much as a taste of it.

Understandably, the convivials of the New World were loathe to relinquish the watering holes of the old. Indeed, so determined were they to have one in proximity that the tavern was made to double as the Town Hall and, after the first road system was established, laws were passed penalizing townships that neglected to provide one. The taverns that served primarily as roadstops for the wagoners and drovers were one-story wooden structures, whereas those catering to

BEL AIR ROYALE
Signature cocktail of the Hotel Bel Air in Los Angeles, the Bel Air Royale combines pink champagne and a shot of peach schnapps to create an effervescent brunch confection.
Combine ingredients in a champagne flute, and garnish with a slice of fresh peach.

125

the gentry were often built of stone and incorporated such refinements as parlors and ballrooms. But whether plain or fancy, their principal commitment was liquid refreshment, and their indispensable feature was a bar.

The Green Dragon Inn, which served, said Daniel Webster, as "headquarters of the revolution," was subsequently conscripted by the Masons for their first Grand Lodge, perhaps by reason of its "remarkable brandy punch." Abbott's in Holden, Massachusetts made its specialty of a flip that, in a quart mug generously laced with whiskey, incorporated egg white and a red hot poker—the one to produce froth, the other to tickle it over the top. Cato's cheerful inn attracted the Knickerbocker crowd to the outskirts of New York for his "excellent beverages that were famous far and wide," according to an historian of the day, "for whether one drank his New York brandy-punch, South Carolina Milk-punch or his Virginia egg-nog which he mixed in single relays by the barrelful, none ever tasted better. He seemed to know just the right number of seconds to beat the separated yolk and egg white, the precise amount of sugar, the exact number of nutmeg grains to be strewn on the mixture, and the right amount of foamy egg white to top it all." And to the south in Virginia, Christina Campbell's Tavern, "where all the best people resorted," as related by a visitor from France, gained an outstanding reputation and loyal following for its table and beverages; George Washington, according to his diary of 1772, stopped there ten times within less than eight weeks.

As nineteenth-century America moved into gilded prosperity, the cheering flips and punches of colonial days evolved into

the zesty mixed spirits of bonanza exuberance: the Brandy Sour, invented in 1841; the Tom Collins, in 1858; the Manhattan, 1874. The tavern remained as a country outpost to refresh the weary traveller, but the serious drinking action moved on to the burgeoning cities. The captains of finance, having despoiled Europe's *chateaux* of their furnishings and its restaurants of their chefs, were accommodated by establishments of the high standing to which they had so recently accustomed themselves. Out West the mining tycoons sought out gussied-up versions of the barrooms of Carson City, refulgent saloons with mirrored bars, shiny railings, plush settees and the ubiquitous painting of Venus taking her bath.

From all corners of the nation these new drinking emporia entered into competition for the emerging palate, and the railroad barons were standing ready to provide transportation to all of them. The grand parlor cars of the Silver Chief and De Luxe wheeled the newly-fortuned to Boston, where they could hobnob with old money at the Parker House, whose French chef devised such meritorious sauces that they were bottled and shipped throughout all of New England, and whose German baker launched lemon meringue, the Boston Cream Pie and those yeasty delights that would gain world renown as Parker House Rolls. More appealing to the single gentlemen about town was the hotel's bar, famed for its plump Wellfleet oysters and exotic confections like the Sangaree, the Gin Sling and the Timber Doodle, so popular with Ivy Leaguers as to provoke the noted essayist Artemis Ward to observe that "Harvard University was pleasantly and conveniently situated in the barroom of Parker's."

127

TOM COLLINS

A Collins is essentially a tall and sour fizz made with soda water, citrus juice and sugar. The Tom Collins, namesake of the fabled bartender of the Planter's Hotel in St. Louis, was invented in 1858. About a century later, it was adapted to new standards of taste in the form of the now-popular Vodka Collins. An original Tom Collins is most properly prepared using Old Tom Gin, a sweeter predecessor of London Dry Gin.

In an ice-filled collins glass, combine two shots of gin or vodka, two of lemon juice and one teaspoon of sugar syrup. Top with soda water, and garnish with a cherry and an orange slice. Serve with a straw.

If they proceeded south to New Orleans, the more adventurous might sample Antoine's Café Brulot and enjoy the heady experience of a Ramos Gin Fizz, while those on the spa circuit might descend on Sulphur Springs to partake of the waters by day and its more flavorful liquids by night. The cream of Southern society who praised the White Hotel's Hailstorm Julep included Governor Zebulon Vance of North Carolina, who in that venerable lobby made his famous remark to Governor Wade Hampton of South Carolina: "It's a damn long time between drinks."

Refreshed, the travellers could continue on to McMakin's Hotel in Jackson, Mississippi, whose proprietor would bellow, "Gentlemen, don't neglect my liquors. *Gentlemen, we are a great people!*" They could drink their way west via the southern route, stopping in for a flavor of sour mash whiskey and card games at Judge Roy Bean's barroom—which doubled as the courthouse—in Langtry, Texas. The more genteel headed for St. Louis, home of Southern Comfort and the Planter's Hotel, whose bartender Tom Collins had just created the cocktail that bears his name, a zesty combination of gin, lemon juice and soda that could hold its own with the hotel's fabled Planter's Punch.

When railing west, the more worldly, such as J. P. Morgan and Andrew Carnegie, preferred to break journey at Rector's in Chicago, which had developed an illustrious Whiskey Sour to whet the appetite for its renowned haute cuisine. From there the thirsty wanderer could detour north via the Clipper Shade Saloon in Butte, Montana, where Molly Demurska, queen of the underworld, tied the knot with the town's marshall, Jack

Jolly, and rode off into the sunset in the town's fire engine; and Erikson's Saloon in Portland, Oregon with its 684-foot long bar, its five-thousand-dollar pipe organ and a ladies orchestra prudently cordoned off by an electrically-charged railing.

Upon arriving in San Francisco, they convened at the bar of the massive marble and brick Palace Hotel, whose staff of one hundred and fifty was the largest in the world, and whose chefs boasted they could satisfy every visitor with specialties from his country. The guest book listed Paderewski, Caruso, Kipling and the Prince of Siam among those who had tested their claim, while the hotel bills of Generals Sherman and Grant and Presidents Hayes, Harrison and McKinley recorded their decidedly stronger interests in the fine wines and brandy cordials that were offered until dawn in the elegant salons.

As America moved through its Gilded Age, virtually every city in the nation boasted a first class emporium, from the well-appointed hotel bars of Boston's Ritz Carlton, Chicago's Atlantic and San Diego's Coronado to flamboyant palaces like Brown's Hotel in Denver, where Evelyn Walsh McLean, reported in the columns as "waving the Hope diamond she had bought from Cartier on its necklace like a yo-yo," liked to throw Sunday night suppers of caviar and champagne for intimate groups of a hundred, and whose advertising boasted that "Theodore Roosevelt once occupied the whole eighth floor suite on learning that our champagne cocktails were frothed from Mumm's Extra Dry."

Entering the twentieth century, New York took center stage with lavish establishments whose focus was expressly on public conviviality. The one thousand guest rooms of the Waldorf-

Astoria emptied onto three floors of public parlors and a block-long corridor dubbed "Peacock Alley" for the fashionable crowd that liked to show off there. A scant decade later the Plaza made its bid with a gilded ballroom, a paneled bar, a richly-upholstered restaurant-cafe and a lobby whose frantic activity attracted a wild mix of royals, parvenues and performers desirous of getting their names in the papers.

In these vast public courts of midtown hospitality, women of the moneyed elite felt comfortable drinking in public for the first time. Until then, the wives of Fifth Avenue had sipped their cocktails at home, in keeping with the tone set by the Van Rensselaers and the Vanderbilts. But as the newly-emergent cafe society swept them into the novel company of foreigners, playboys and ladies of the lighter stage, it became increasingly acceptable to be seen dining out. The new restaurants, ever mindful of a lucrative clientele, were quick to install the smoky mirrors and flattering pink lighting that set off to advantage the ladies' jewels and complexions.

Their husbands took kindly to gastronomic equality, but held fast to their fellowship of drinking together in the sanctuary of the bar. On their way home from work they still stopped in at the Knickerbocker Hotel for a Martini and conversation under the Maxfield Parrish "Old King Cole"; after hours they liked to convene for a nightcap at the bars of the newer hotels, the Pierre, the St. Regis and the Savoy.

None was ever busier, however, than the Men's Bar at the Waldorf, said by some to be the greatest of its kind, whose barkeeps prided themselves on their relationships with their customers. "When you order your brand," as one regular

PLANTER'S PUNCH
Credit for this delicious sour-based punch is accorded to both Tom Collins, fabled bartender at the Planter's Hotel in St. Louis and the creator of many now-standard cocktails, and to a 19th-century Jamaican planter's wife who supposedly first offered the formula of one part sour, two parts sweet, three parts strong and four parts weak as an antidote to the island's heat.

Planter's Punch is made by combining lemon juice, sugar syrup, dark rum and water in the above proportions over ice in a shaker. Shake vigorously and pour, without straining, into a goblet or collins glass. Decorate with fresh fruit. One standard variation calls for a dash of Angostura bitters, another for a dash of grenadine.

recorded it, "the bartender places the bottle with the face of the label towards you so that you can see it and know what you are getting. He will offer to pour it for you, but if you want, you can pour it yourself, and after the signal will walk away and leave the bottle in front of you." One of these described the action toward late afternoon, when men would come in "to get outside of a drink…Everyone struggles to get a foot on the brass rail that runs around the bottom of the bar. Sometimes the gang is ten deep, all straining toward that common goal."

The Men's Bar was home away from home to untold numbers of the powerful and famous; Mark Twain, "Gentleman Jim" Corbett—so called because he always left a tip—who had his own saloon up the street, and to "Buffalo Bill" Cody, whose reply to offers of free drinks became as much his trademark as his wide-brimmed hat and Prince Albert coat. "Sir," he would say, "you speak the language of my tribe."

It was at the Waldorf Bar that the free lunch, that gastronomic outgrowth of earlier bardom's deployment of salty snacks to whet the whistles of its clients, reached its zenith in a spread that cost the hotel the enormous sum of over seventy-five hundred dollars yearly. "No menu in puzzling French to mystify or confuse. The uninitiate saw what he saw, and what he fancied he could sample at his leisure. And spread out for his delectation—for he was free to choose, and to whatever extent—were light and savory canapés, thirst-provoking anchovies in various tinted guises, and other delicacies; and there were substantial slices of beef or ham, ordinary as well as Virginia, and a wonderful assortment of cheeses of robust odors;

PINK LADY

No roster of Jazz-Age confections would be complete without the Pink Lady, which owes its unusually smooth, sweet and dry flavor to the inclusion of a frothed egg white.

In a shaker, combine cracked ice, one part grenadine, two parts lemon juice, two parts apple brandy, and half an egg white. Shake vigorously, and then add half of a total of six parts gin. Shake again, and add the remaining gin. Shake a third time, and strain into a chilled cocktail glasses.

not forgetting the crisp radishes and sprightly, delicate spring onions, and olives stuffed and unstuffed."

Thus might American drinking have settled sedately into a Martini at the Knickerbocker, Juleps at the Old White, a Bronx with free lunch at the Waldorf and champagne with everything everywhere had it not been for the war across the world that shook up genteel expectations of a predictable tomorrow. Then, following too hard on the champagne celebrations of 1918, came the gag of Prohibition; like an ill-fitting cork in the explosive ferment of post-war euphoria, the Volstead Act served as the starting gun for the Roaring Twenties.

On that black day of January 16, 1920, as those meddling ladies of temperance toasted each other in lemonade, the rest of the nation collapsed into mourning. That last Sunday night across the nation, thousands of automobiles clogged the streets, disgorging desperate revelers into restaurants and clubs, whose two-dollar tables were going for fifty dollars and up and whose last liquor was going for whatever it would fetch. New York staged elaborate obsequies. The Park Avenue Hotel draped its tables in black. The clientele of Reisenweber's Cafe was invited to a funeral ball at which six waiters paraded with a coffin to Chopin's "Funeral March." The Golden Blade Restaurant, known for its ice skating extravaganzas, glided a coffin around the dance floor to collect bottles and glasses. By midnight the mourners had shed their last tear, and by dawn the nation's eyes were dry.

Not so, however, its saloons. Never slow to react to an inactive cash register, the Great American Bar poured out its

woes to the first concerned listener and, by the most profitable grace of its new best friend the bootlegger, rose again as a speakeasy. By 1925 there were thought to be 100,000 "speaks" in New York City alone, with 52nd Street reportedly the wettest in the country. "WYBMADIITY," read a sign in the popular Dizzy Club, and if you asked the bartender what it meant, he answered "Will you buy me a drink if I tell you?" The answer was yes, always yes.

The better-heeled generally avoided the drinking dens downtown, a labyrinth of nefarious dives whose illicit alcohols killed almost seven hundred of the unsuspecting in one year alone. Anita Loos recalled nights on the blue town with the indomitable Mencken: "Neither Menck nor his group ever examined any drink too closely and, as our friendship progressed in the various speakeasies of Manhattan, I found that they all drank freely of bathtub gin, whiskey colored with creosote, and beer that was needled with ether."

The high-toned speaks of midtown had to be more careful, of course; they were catering to the big nobs like financier Gilbert Kahn and publisher Ogden Reid. Here reigned Jack and Charlie's, which safeguarded reputations of such eminent Prohibition holdouts as Robert Benchley, Bea Lillie, Dorothy Parker and Ben Hecht by its ingenious four-alarm warning system and a bar that folded its contents into the cellar at the touch of a button. At closing time, patrons were sent home with pre-packaged bottles of Bronxes, Gin Rickeys, Martinis, Whiskey Sours, Daiquiris, Pink Ladies, Bacardis and Sidecars—the drinks that would go down in history as the "cocktails of the twenties."

140

Other neighborhood hangouts were Moriarty's, Bleecks and the Brooks Club, which never closed. There was Leon and Eddie's, whose entrance sign read, "Through These Portals The Most Beautiful Girls In The World Pass Out"; the Town Casino Club, whose fountain featured a fulsome bather frolicking *au naturel* in jets of neon water; the Merry-Go-Round, where the upper crust liked to sip cocktails in formal attire as they circled the dance floor astride wooden horses; the tasteful Deauville, which had undergone a gilded transformation from Isadora Duncan's residence to a cafe whose Limoges cups held spiked tea, and where members had to flash a gold card to gain entrance.

No such nicety was demanded by speakeasy queen Belle Livingston, the hefty two-time divorcée of a Cleveland millionaire and an Italian Count. She charged a steep five-dollar entry fee to her plush five-story Country Club on East 58th Street, where she played hostess in her red satin pajamas and, when customers displeased her, acted as her own bouncer.

A rival claimant for the royal title was Texas Guinan, a boisterous blonde from Waco who favored ermine and greeted the customers of her 45th Street club with the raucous "Hello, Sucker" that became the catch phrase of the dry years. When business was slow, she would clap her hands loudly and yell "Order up!"

And order up they did, there and everywhere else. By the mid-twenties, when the *New York Telegram* assigned a team of reporters to research the availability of liquor in Manhattan, they were able to buy it in "dancing academies, drugstores, delicatessens, cigar stores, confectionaries, soda fountains, barbershops, beauty parlors, paint stores, malt shops, fruit stands, groceries, athletic clubs, grillrooms, tearooms, boarding houses, laundries, social clubs, spaghetti houses."

This was flask liquor, of course, carried on the hip and quaffed on the run, courtesy of bootleggers who gave more thought to profits than to quality. The more established among them, such as George Cassiday, the green-hatted supplier to Capitol Hill, prided themselves on potable alcohols that could be dispensed straight from a seltzer bottle, but the stuff that was issued by Al Capone and his ilk was for the most part so nasty that no decent speak could expect it to pass through the portals of a customer's esophagus unless it was first doctored with the syrups and sodas that expanded so colorfully the repertoire of the cocktail.

Things weren't very different out West, although California had some catching up to do. Two short decades earlier Los Angeles was still country; people came for the beaches and the climate, not for carousing. So restricted was its nightlife that when the Hollywood Hotel opened in 1903 dancing was permitted only on Thursday nights and alcohol not at all.

It fell to the fledgling movie industry to launch social drinking in southern California. The silent-screen bevy met up with Gloria Swanson and Jack Warner at the cocktail bar of the Alexander Hotel, with its "million-dollar carpet," so called for the deals that were made on it. They hung out on Spring Street, ending up at the block-long Imperial Bar, where you could roll dice and purchase lottery tickets between drinks. But even there the action folded early, under the watchful eye of the growing temperance movement. Only in 1912, when

Baron Long opened the Vernon Club on the outskirts of town, hiring Rudolph Valentino as a tango dancer and importing the first jazz bands, did Hollywood have an all-out nightspot.

The new night life was glamorous and fun, and the stars never looked back. They danced to the beat of Lionel Hampton and Duke Ellington. They boogied and they shimmied, learned the Chicken Shuffle and the Charleston, and streamed into the vast dance halls that had sprung up along the coast to show off their new dance steps; the Egyptian, where Harold Lloyd and Bebe Daniels won a trophy for best dance partners, and the Sunset Inn, which had parking for over three thousand cars and offered "free cocktails, live cabaret, souvenirs, favors and dancin' til dawn."

Hollywood met Prohibition with characteristic flamboyance, inventing new drinks and places to flaunt them. The illegal hootch dropped off shore by rum runners ended up in the Shark's Tooth, the Rum Smash and the Panama Cooler that became the below-the-table specialties of the Kit Kat Club, Monkey Farm, Midnight Follies and Sneak Inn, holes in the wall with the longevity of ice cubes.

Celebrities interested in higher visibility sought out more reputable purveyors of illegal fun. They flocked to the Plantation Cafe, where spirituous supplies were camouflaged behind art director Cedric Gibbons' dazzling canopy of stars. They convened at the Montmartre, where rumors circulated of a dispensary in the Gents as John Barrymore, Winston Churchill, Robert Young and Prince George of England were observed to be taking an inordinately long time to wash their hands. The ladies had devised a more high-flown solution airily referred to

CLOVER CLUB

This classic of the cocktail era is named for the Clover Club, a popular Hollywood nightspot of the 1930s. It's sweet, frothy flavor charmed the likes of Jean Harlow and Clara Bow, and prompted Fay Wray to claim that the Clover Club cocktail was guaranteed to give one "all the right ideas."

Combine one part grenadine or raspberry syrup, two parts lemon juice and one-half of an egg white in a shaker with cracked ice. Shake until blended and creamy, then add eight parts gin. Shake again, and strain into a chilled cocktail glass.

as the Flying Luncheon, whereby Mrs. Fatty Arbuckle, Mabel Normand and company would head for an airfield after the entrée and take a spin off the coast in an aircraft well stocked with champagne.

By the end of the twenties, nothing remained of Prohibition in Hollywood but the increased importance of drinking. So ingenious were the new impressarios at stocking Jazz-Age entertainments with provisions for the parched that Repeal might have seemed anticlimactic but for their resolve to keep the movie crowd hopping.

They had to contend with the Depression, of course, but there were enough profits from the new talkies to warrant celebration. While the barflies of Raymond Chandler's novels nursed their lone whiskeys on the barstools of Vine and Hollywood, Tinseltown kicked up its heels at a flurry of new nightspots. The queues along Sunset Boulevard weren't for soup kitchens, but for the delicacies of The Vendome, the latest "place to dine." While waiting for delicious things to be done with goose livers and Edam in sauterne, Mae West, the Clark Gables and Marlene Dietrich "freshened up," as reported in the columns, with "a daisy called the 'Vendome Special Sling' ($1) in which the bartender makes magic out of ginger beer, cherry brandy, gin and lime juice."

Racier establishments also sprang up. At the Colony Club, Gary Cooper, Jean Harlow and the irrepressible Clara Bow—her red hair set aflame by an emerald dress, orange gloves and a mass of rhinestone buckles—spiced their Rickeys with roulette, before negotiating the steep ramp to the Clover Club, whose

enticing cocktail by that name was guaranteed, said Fay Wray of *King Kong* fame, to give you "all the right ideas."

As Hollywood matured and moved toward the forties, the stars became more selective about where they wanted to be seen. They chose places for their music, keeping step with the times in dance palaces like the Palomar and the Avalon, where the giants of jazz made way for the Big Bands of swing, Jimmy Dorsey and "King of Swing" Benny Goodman.

They chose places for their atmosphere. To make it in the thirties a club had to have decor. Top architects were called in; Gordon Kaufman's *tour de force* for Earl Carroll's seated one thousand people in luxurious comfort against a backdrop of black patent leather and gold neon. Wayne McAllister remodelled the ballroom of the Biltmore into "the world's largest nightclub," placing the begowned and bejewelled on wide, floating balconies where they might sip their fizzes at an elegant remove from the dance floor.

For a taste of the tropics there was Hawaiian Paradise, themed around bamboo, live parrots and cascading waterfalls that spilled into a fish-stocked pool—as did Jackie Gleason, by his lady friend's telling of one of their wetter visits.

Finally and foremost, the stars went to places for their cocktails. *Screen Guide* recommended the Brown Derby for its delicious fizzes, its generous highballs and, "if your taster wants teasing," its tempting Bamboo. Exotic cocktails like the Tailless Monkey drew the crowd south to the Zamboanga, billed as "the most beautiful Polynesian paradise in the United States," and to the newly-opened Trocadero, where Betty Grable dipped croissants into her Pink Ladies, while its downstairs

Cellar drew on stronger resources: "Drinks run from 60¢ to $1.50."—*Screen Guide* again—"That one-fifty number, in case you are interested, is a lulu called 'French 75' or T.N.T. By way of warning, it is just that, dynamite."

To draw attention and customers, the trendier clubs strutted their liquid attractions. The Casanova Club hailed its violet-colored Casanova Cocktail; Don the Beachcomber featured the comely Vicious Virgin, the radiant Never Say Die and the Pi Yi, served in a miniature pineapple. Across town the Melody Grill offered sweetly-flavored fizzes like Moist Rhapsody or the bolder Companion's Revenge that served as a nightcap for both the evening and a tedious escort.

Thus did the cocktail in its infinite variety parallel the dance steps of the times. Like the hot beat of jazz, and the successive rhythms of boogie, Charleston, conga and rhumba, which hit for a minute and moved on, so, too, were these exotic cocktails fads of a moment, and the places that sprang up to dispense them were as often as not washed away in the seltzer by morning.

The Second World War would cut short the frivolity. In Hollywood the last glorious hurrah of 1940 saw the opening of the Mocambo and the million-dollar Palladium, where Barbara Stanwyck, Gary Cooper, Judy Garland and Bing Crosby danced to the sounds of Tommy Dorsey and Glenn Miller. But the revels carried on with the growing realization that the spree was finally over. Swing tapered off, emptying the dance halls; gambling was eventually flushed out to Nevada. Tinseltown settled down to a quieter routine of caviar and Dom Pérignon lunches at Romanoffs, steak and Scotch dinners at Chasen's,

147

and dancing with pale cocktails at a handful of new supper clubs that were designed to shield rather than publicize the presence of a star.

By the time the war was over, the pattern of American drinking had radically altered. Bars held open their doors for the celebrations of returning G. I.s, but society was more inclined to combine cocktails with decorous dining in well-appointed establishments that anticipated the new era with a more subdued atmosphere.

In New York a handful of carryovers from the dry days—the grander of the speaks gone legit—still catered to the crowd of playboys and heiresses. El Morocco carried on the hoopla of twilight till dawn for the high-livers, the out-of-towners and the glamorous internationals just disembarked from HMS *Queen Mary*. Jack and Charlie's had re-emerged as the "21" after the closing party of the century; the more illustrious of its regulars had been invited to destroy whichever piece of Prohibition regalia they had least cared for. Rising to the challenge, Jim Sheffield brought down the chandelier, Gilbert Kahn ripped off the toilet seat and Nick Luddington demolished the door that had once almost demolished him when propelled from within by Ernest Hemingway. After the main stairway was sawn through, cutting off the recruits from liquid supplies, the revelers all walked three blocks uptown to a new address and new times.

The face of the city changed. The El was torn down, leaving only a handful of Third Avenue bars, like Costello's and P.J. Clarke's, to accommodate the old-timers. The cocktail set migrated happily to brighter quarters in the genteel new

lounges born of the post-Repeal resolution never to go underground again. "No longer slinking, respectably drinking, like civilized women and men," read the lyrics of a current hit tune, "Cocktails For Two." Jack and Charlie's new emporium openly catered to the cocktail sophisticates—prompting Rocky Marciano's classic remark, "Can you imagine them letting me into '21'? I'm lucky to count that high"—and Manhattan's tonier establishments followed suit.

Thus *Vanity Fair* would extol the newly-decorated Sherry-Netherland's bar as "one of the most distinctive and agreeable spots in town, whose simple and restful decor remains quietly but pleasantly in the background, setting you off to fine advantage." A few blocks away at the Rainbow Room, New York's ultimate supper club, young romantics ordered Champagne Cocktails from waiters in tails and fox-trotted till dawn on a revolving dance floor to the tunes of an organ that cast rainbows on the ceiling.

At the sedate Algonquin, the *literati* gathered on couches in the lobby and summoned drinks with little bells, as Edmund Wilson grew eloquent and Alec Wilder coined his newest *bon mot*. Later, between acts, the Broadway contingent crowded into the tiny Blue Bar where George Soroko was mixing "the best Martini in town" from Boodles gin, Noilly Prat and "a drop of Pernod to bring out the flavor."

The new cocktail round read like the entries in Noel Coward's diary: "Drinks with Judy Garland at the Carlyle," whose exquisite Bemelmans Bar, with its watercolors by Vertes, set off cocktails like the White Russian and the Fontainbleau Special; "Quick drink with Vivien and Larry at the Plaza," whose Oak Bar now extended its repertoire to exotica like the Pousse L'Amour and the Warsaw Cocktail; "Stopped in at St. Regis for cocktails with Cole," who said their famed Bloody Marys surpassed even Bertin's.

PIMM'S CUP

Pimm's Number One is a spiced gin imported from England. For many, a Pimm's Cup is the drink of choice at summertime events, from Britain's Ascot Derby to America's Fourth of July fireworks.

A Pimm's Cup is made in the standard ratio of one-third Pimm's to two-thirds mix. Suitable mixes include British lemonade—a bubbly soda for which there is no U.S. equivalent—ginger ale or lemon-lime soda. Finishing touches for this heavily-garnished drink include, but are not limited to, cucumber slices and orange wedges.

If all this seemed too genteel, those who still felt like kicking up their heels could always head over to Europe. The vast dance halls of the *belle epoque*, which had been consecrated to the absinthe extravagances of Montmartre so well chronicled by Toulouse-Lautrec, had long since given way to small smoky *boîtes*. Erik Satie worked as second pianist at the racy Chat Noire, walking around with a hammer in his pocket for protection. The Boeuf sur le Toit, an eccentric cabaret designed by Cocteau and Milhaud, attracted the new internationals—Stravinsky, Serge Lifar, Arthur Rubinstein and the monocled Diaghilev, whose famous injunction to Cocteau, "Astonish me!" would set the tone for the era.

By the 1930s, "cocktail" was assimilated into the Parisian vocabulary, along with "up-to-date," "shimmy" and "le jazz hot." Attention focussed on Bricktop's, the first club in Paris to serve cocktails at the tables, an inspiration of Cole Porter. As the club's self-designated godfather, he called in Hoyningen-Huene to do the lighting, squired Bricktop herself around town in a Molyneux gown to drum up publicity and wrote the sultry "Miss Otis Regrets" for her opening number. His habit of sitting at the piano far into the night and Bricktop's flamboyant personality brought in a luminous clientele. T. S. Eliot wrote a poem for the flaming-haired cabaret singer; the Prince of Wales threw the opening party. Grace Moore never failed to grab the microphone—a practice Shirley MacLaine would repeat years later—and Scott Fitzgerald wrote of it as the place he had spent "so much time and so much money." Gloria Swanson, who sailed off from Bricktop's after her marriage to the Marquis de la Falaise, wired back: "How would you like to go on your honeymoon and have your husband say 'I'll be so happy to get back to Brick's.'?"

For the most part the art crowd preferred Montparnasse, where they could people-watch on the overflowing terraces of the famous trio of cafes. The writers gravitated to the Select, where newsman Harold Stearns sat until dawn; "a silly life," he wrote in retrospect, "and I have missed it every day since." Artists frequented the Rotonde, where Picasso would appear on a Sunday in the company of Matisse and Derain. And in-evitably, whether for breakfast, lunch or dinner or all these plus a nightcap, everyone passed through the Dôme, the heart and the nervous system of the expatriate colony, who checked in for messages and news of what was happening in the world— "the American cathedral of sophistication," Sinclair Lewis once called it. He stopped in often enough for his Calvados and Kir, but perhaps not when Kiki was jumping on the tables to catch the eye of Man Ray. Ezra Pound dropped in frequently, and for a while Hemingway, too, but he soon tired of aspiring writers who began going there "to be seen publicly as a daily substi-tute for immortality," and moved on to the Trois et As, where diminutive blonde poet Edna St. Vincent Millay matched him drink for drink as she listened raptly to his bull and fish stories.

Hemingway's drinking route progressed through three dec-ades from the Closerie des Lilas in the old Latin Quarter, where he drank whisky with James Joyce, to the Jockey Club, whose outer walls were painted with cowboys and Indians by Hilaire Hiler and whose inner life was jumping with black bands and bohemia; "best orchestra, best drinks, a wonderful clientele and the world's most beautiful women." The allusion may have

PIÑA COLADA
When Puerto Rico's La Barrachina Restaurant and Caribe Hilton each claimed that the Piña Colada was invented behind its bar, the ensuing controversy received more than a passing reference in food or travel columns. Front page headlines in the *San Juan Star* reflected just how much interest and devotion this local treasure inspired. Drawing upon the fruitful bounty of the island, the Piña Colada's creamy, pineapple-coconut flavor is well suited for summertime entertainments.

Combine a shot of rum, two shots of pineapple juice, one-half shot of cream of coconut and one-half shot of cream in a blender filled with cracked ice. Blend and serve in a large goblet, garnished with a pineapple slice and a cherry.

been to Josephine Baker, of the gold-lacquered fingernails, slinky black sheath and turban made of bananas, with whom he had danced throughout one memorable night. "Wasn't til the joint closed she told me she had nothing on underneath."

There was even a moment when Hemingway liked Harry's New York Bar, clubhouse for so many Americans in Paris, birthplace of the Bloody Mary and, some say, the Sidecar. As the bar gained notoriety for its address, *5 Rue Daunou*—drawled out as "sank roo da noo"—for its revolving dispenser serving "chiens chauds" and, once word of its eight hundred cocktails reached the college crowd, for its wallful of pennants, Hemingway pronounced it "overquaint," and moved on to the Ritz, social nexus of the *Rive Droit*, whose Cambon and Little Bar had become the gathering ground of the international set.

The imbibers of the Right Bank were the drinking world's cosmopolites, a group of sophisticates who could drink with ease anywhere. In London they patronized the Dorchester, behind whose familiar facade, backdrop to so many musicals, performed Roy and his famous Martinis. They felt right at home at the Savoy, renowned in Edwardian days for its seventy bathrooms—its closest rival had only four—for its Pêche Melba, created for the diva by its legendary chef Escoffier—and for its service: "Please command anything," read a note on each guest's door, "from a cup of tea to a cocktail, and it will come up in the twinkling of an Embankment lamp." To that illustrious reputation were added the accolades for its American Bar, so called because it was the first in Europe to chill Martinis and because its bartender, Harry Craddock, had shaken cocktails for Teddy Roosevelt and John L. Sullivan in pre-Prohibition New

156

York. Craddock's supreme invention, the White Lady, must have held a fateful attraction, since by the 1930s the Savoy was known as the 49th State. John Barrymore, Norma Talmadge and Marion Davies succumbed to the pale lady's charm. Only Caruso resisted; when asked for his drink request by the legendary barkeep, the world's greatest tenor put his finger to his lips and whispered, "Mumm's the word." So wide was the American Bar's appeal that in 1947, the year the bar was opened to the ladies, George Bernard Shaw could assert that he was the only male celebrity never to have set foot on its brass rail.

By the fifties the drinking trail was fully international. The gambling set gravitated to Monte Carlo, where they liked to recover from a depleting night at the casino with a refreshing Bloody Mary on the terrace of the Hôtel de Paris. Here they could marvel at the sensibility and extravagance of Prince Apraxine, who liked to order strawberries out of season, crush them with a fork that their fragrance might permeate his champagne, and return them uneaten. With such a gilded clientele the hotel's bartender was especially inspired to create titled drinks, a talent that once earned him the gratuity of a gold cigarette case from the Maharajah of Rajpipla and the gratitude of the deposed Prince Alfonso, whose morale was tactfully restored by the drink which bore his name, a delightful new confection based on Dubonnet and gin, though the Prince himself was a Bourbon.

Here as elsewhere, the bartender had come to be as much of a draw as the bar. Few ever passed by St. Moritz without paying their respects to Gustav, who had been boosting the spirits of the rich and the royal for a quarter of a century. In Brussels, the Metropole merited a detour for the creations of Gus Tops, who dispensed his profile on silk handkerchiefs, together with recipes of his masterworks, the Tops Smile, the Black Russian and the Wild Dry.

No visitor to Athens could pass up the chance to raise a glass with Jean Pallis, who earned the coveted title of Head Barman of the prestigious Grande Bretagne for forty years service in the bar he immortalized in the gin, angostura, and apricot brandy delight that constitute the ineffable No. 1 G. B.

Harry's Bar had branched out to Rome, and at lunchtime it was such a must, thanks to Cipriani's famous Bellinis, that the Aga Khan moved his residence from the Grand Hotel to the Bauer so that he could walk there without crossing a bridge. Evenings unfolded in the burnished mahogany of the Grand Hotel Bar, whose legendary barlord, Mauro Lotti, would invent Italy's most famous nightcap, the Vodka Imperiale, which combined every fruit in season, except those that might stain the drink red, with vodka and maraschino liqueur. Peter Sellers, Richard Burton and Peter O'Toole responded to its charms, and the bar's crowd to theirs. "They would tell each other stories far into the night," Lotti recalls, "and everyone was so entertained they forgot to order a drink."

Back in Paris, Frank Meier had reigned for twenty-six years at the Ritz bar, where he introduced such sophisticated clients as Coco Chanel, King Ferdinand of Romania and the Duke of Sutherland to some of America's greatest cocktails: the Bee's Knees, the Whizz Bang and the Golden Slipper. His successors,

Georges and Bertin, carried on through the forties, naming cocktails for their more illustrious customers; the Caruso, the Prince of Wales and the Sea Pea—for Cole Porter's initials. On his re-entry into Paris as a military correspondent, Hemingway made the Ritz his first stop, to "liberate the cellars," in return for which courtesy the Little Bar was renamed in his honor the Hemingway Bar.

The crowd of the Ritz was the crowd of the world. They girdled the earth seeking ever more exotic libations. In Singapore it was for the alluring Gin Sling that Somerset Maugham and Douglas Fairbanks lingered on the terrace of the Raffles Hotel far into the sunset. In Shanghai it was the Casanova Club's exquisite signature drink that so enraptured Bea Wells. "Take along a cherry colored gown and white clips for your hair," she wrote nostalgically, "and order a Caresse Cocktail, a house special created of gin and cherry brandy, Cognac and Curaçao. A small Hawaiian band will be playing 'La Cucaracha' and you will find yourself wishing that a square polished dance floor were the length and breadth of the world."

THE LIFE OF THE PARTY

"A very merry, dancing, drinking, laughing, quaffing
and unthinking time."
—John Dryden

Christmas, New Year's, birthdays, weddings. The convivial have always welcomed an occasion
to come together for a drink. The popping of corks and clinking of tumblers, air redolent with
the fragrance of hot rum and lemon, wassail bowls filled to the brim with smoking gin and mulled
ale, have long symbolized that great unifying social ritual, the party. The celebrations of the Old
World bore no resemblance to the cocktail party as the twentieth century came to invent it, but
spirited confections were indispensable to them all. The proverbial punch whose brewing inspired
such grand theater in the novels of Dickens and the plum pudding set alight in brandy that
warmed what might have been Tiny Tim's last Christmas on earth had performed equally warmly
in the festivities of the New World. In those early times, people came together irrespective of the
hour to sample heady potables irrespective of the occasion. A parson's visit was reason enough
to partake of a fine Madeira, and each household stood at the ready to devote hours or days to
the confection of the cheering punches of the weddings, banquets and dancing assemblies that
took over the taverns within and without. John Hancock may not have made history as a host,
but at a party he gave in 1792 he regaled two hundred guests with one hundred thirty-six bowls
of punch and three hundred bottles of wine, plus sherry and brandy cordials for dessert.

The great imbibers of the Gilded Age held no less closely to their celebrations. The newly-
moneyed magnificos roistered about town, joining public entertainments at the old-time saloons
that offered free Tom and Jerrys at Christmas and New Year's. Even the least Irish of them stopped

POUSSE CAFE

A sweet and elegant after-dinner cordial, there are as many variations to the Pousse Cafe as there are liqueurs and flavored syrups. When building a Pousse Cafe, take note that the density of each ingredient is as important as its flavor or color in determining the success of this stratified work of art. Since each layer must sit neatly upon the layer beneath it, the heavier layers must go on the bottom. There is no table of densities for liqueurs, since the same product may vary from distillery to distillery, but the rule of thumb is the higher the proof the lower the density, with non-alcoholic syrups such as grenadine being generally the heaviest.

A standard Pousse Cafe might contain grenadine, Chartreuse, crème de cacao, crème de menthe and brandy, poured in that order. To achieve the perfect layering, pour very carefully, either down the side of the cordial glass or over the back of a spoon.

in at McGinty's on St. Patrick's Day, when so much free whiskey was dispensed that one year Tom Heath, its most distinguished regular, ate the shamrocks on the bar, thinking they were watercress.

When dining out, the nabobs liked to entertain extravagantly at their clubs or the grander establishments that knew how to throw a party of consequence. "Diamond Jim" Brady gave a banquet at New York's Holland House to commemorate the closing of his unprofitable stables at which the five hundred bottles of Mumm's that were consumed were poured by waiters clad in his racing colors. Leonard Jerome, the grandfather of Winston Churchill, had twenty barmen in attendance for one banquet he gave at Delmonico's, best remembered by the ladies present for the gold bracelet each received.

Meanwhile, the matrons of Fifth Avenue, cued by the stiff upper back of Regina Victoria, corseted domestic activity between the whalebones of proper luncheons, genteel dinners and that new ceremony imported from England, the afternoon tea. Not that these structured entertainments were any less liquid. Tea for the straight-laced was often laced straight, as witnessed by the cheerful afternoon gatherings on Nob Hill in the drawing room of sugar heiress Mrs. Alfred Spreckels, whose massive silver teapot was known to dispense the finest Ceylon, diluted with gin. The Joseph O'Donahues of New York shipping wealth, noted for their sobriety, nevertheless prided themselves on their table. Every week they were in residence, they would import an expert from the venerable firm of Bellows and Company to select and decant the formidable sequence of sherries, wines, champagnes, ports and brandies destined for

their Sunday night collations. These small family affairs acquired *éclat* from guests like Sarah Bernhardt, whose arrival with her pet lion on one such occasion provoked near mutiny in the world of upstairs-downstairs when the butler refused to remove the beast's sealskin overcoat. Even the stilted receptions at Newport, where *the* Mrs. Astor took the last stand on matters of protocol, might have been faulted for formality but never for a scarcity of spirituous beverages.

Widely as they were distributed, mixed drinks had still not become the center of social attraction. It was only when three new ingredients were poured into the shaker, namely the rise of the new hoi polloi, the institution of the 9:00 to 5:00 working day and, most markedly, the passage of the Volstead Act, that the specific time slot called the cocktail hour, with its attendant parties and people, came into existence.

In the uncertain world of the turn of the century, when one no longer knew next to whom one might sit, it was safer, at supper parties, after-dinner receptions or that handy novelty, the buffet, to stand—and preferably in groups large enough that one might amuse oneself with the novel company of a chorus girl or a rake without being constrained, heaven forbid, to shake hands.

Safest of all, of course, was simply to stay home, a turn of social events promoted by Heublein's, which had introduced the first bottled cocktails in the 1890s with the promise of a "better cocktail than is served in any bar in the world." For the first time the mixed drink displayed its charm on working America, as householders on Main Street and in the suburbs, newly adapted to an eight-hour day that precluded the nicety of afternoon tea, welcomed the new chic of cocktails at home, on the patio or by the fire.

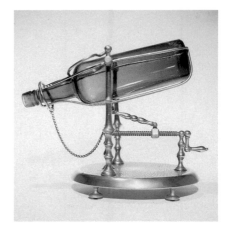

There was still, however, no consecration of an hour, no extended time frame allotted specifically to drinking. Cocktails were confined to a single Manhattan or one very small Martini wedged into the quarter hour before going on to dinner.

The cocktail's longer moment came when Prohibition drove party drinking into the home, bringing women openly into the drinking ritual and enhancing the art of amateur mixology. Ever since J. P. Morgan had confected an eccentric concoction of rum, Curaçao and Chartreuse, which he called, for no reason he could ever make clear, an Alamagoozlum, tinkering with a chemistry set of bartools and flammable liquids had been the acceptable hobby of a gentleman. Now, however, that the host was perforce his own bartender, it became a matter of necessity and social one-upmanship to offer a unique and appealing creation. Since the preparation of a cocktail craved an audience, and the larger the better, it was discovered in the course of invention that amusing mixes of alcohol attracted amusing mixes of people.

Heightening the fun was the element of risk. In defiance of the iniquitous Eighteenth Amendment, cocktail parties became the exciting, flagrant, daring thing to do.

Thus the cocktail party was launched, never to look back, and suddenly, it seemed simultaneously, the cocktail phenomenon was everywhere: smart cocktail receptions like those the Henry Swopes threw at Prospect Point for such of the Long Island Sunday sporty set as John Hay Whitney, Scott Fitzgerald and Harpo Marx, who liked to sneak behind the butler and

TOM AND JERRY

The Tom and Jerry, like the Martini, is attributed to bartender "Professor" Jerry Thomas, who claimed credit for inventing it behind the bar of San Francisco's El Dorado.

A Tom and Jerry is prepared in a two-step process. First mix a batter by separately beating the yolk and white of one egg, then combine it with enough powdered sugar to make the mixture stiffen. Add a pinch of baking soda, a quarter-ounce of rum and a little more sugar so that the mixture remains stiff.

When it's time to serve the drink, dissolve one tablespoon of the batter in three tablespoons of hot milk in a warm mug. Add one and one-half ounces of rum, then fill the mug with hot milk. Top with a float of brandy and a sprinkle of nutmeg. Traditionally associated with Thanksgiving and Christmas, Tom and Jerrys have become a standard at ski resorts and winter playgrounds.

switch the names under the cocktail orders on his tray; literary cocktail parties in the George Kaufmans' salon where George Gershwin, Moss Hart, and Edna Ferber would be asked "Tea or a drink?" or in the studios of Greenwich Village, which featured chanted versions of poetry then current, with Vachel Lindsay's "The Congo" adjudged the most compatible with the rhythm of a cocktail shaker.

The cocktail party sailed over to Europe, tripping into London on the heels of America's more emancipated emissaries: Tallulah Bankhead, who enjoyed shocking duchesses with cartwheels around the room and receiving dukes at the intimate cocktail parties she liked to give from her bath; and Laura Corrigan, whose chief party trick was standing on her head, and who instructed her butler, when she took up residence in London, to "give a cocktail to everyone who comes to the door."

The English were not immediately seduced. They were still making the acquaintance of White Ladies at afternoon garden parties, given generally on weekends and often, at a time when political decisions were made in country houses, by the formidable Lady Grenville. Her memory lives on for the note she once placed on the tray of her inebriated butler which read, "You are very drunk, please go home," and which he promptly swung around and presented to the Prime Minister.

Londoners found it difficult to push back tea at 4:30 to cocktails at 6:00. Alec Waugh recorded an attempt in 1924 by the very well-connected Nevinsons, who "decided that it might be a good time at which to give a party and sent out an announcement that they were emerging from their winter

retirement and would be at home on the last Saturday in April between five and seven. Questioned, years afterwards, they were vague as to the number of invitations they sent out; but some thirty glasses were arranged beside a large earthenware jug containing a yellow, coolish but not cold mixture, in which rum was the chief ingredient. Only two guests arrived. The Londoners of the Nevinsons' acquaintance—and the Nevinsons touched life at many points—were puzzled by the novelty of the invitation."

In Paris the cocktail party found the barricades already lowered by the *grandes horizontales*, those cocottes and courtesans who had long since invaded the sanctuary of Proust's lingering aristocracy. The *haut monde* moved readily into the swirl of an epoch that dined extravagantly at Maxim's, danced on the tables of Montmartre, dressed in the loud colors Poiret had borrowed from Bakst and gave wild entertainments.

The most notorious of these lustrous amusements, thrown by the new money of M. et Mme. Natanson, would have preempted the first cocktail parties by nearly a decade, had it not started after eight. Toulouse-Lautrec tended bar that night—which lasted till dawn—standing chin-high before a sign that read in English "Don't Speak To The Man At The Wheel." He concocted, at his estimate, two thousand cocktails, among them elaborate, layered drinks of red, green and yellow liqueurs, and surreal inventions of sardines and gin set alight in long silver dishes.

Kees van Dongen, that most Parisian of Dutch artists, himself a great giver of eccentric entertainments, described those years as "the cocktail epoch. Cocktails! They are of all colours.

172

They contain something of everything. No, I do not merely mean the cocktails that one drinks. They are symbolic of the rest. The modern society woman is a cocktail. She is a bright mixture. Society itself is a bright mixture. You can blend people of all tastes and classes. The cocktail epoch!"

Even van Dongen might have been startled at what poured from the shaker once the Americans brought over their idea of a party. The command performance staged for women friends by Nathalie Bryher, "that wild girl from Cincinnati," for which she had hired Mata Hari to ride in half-clad on a white horse, was a mere curtain-opener to the extravaganzas that fired Elsa Maxwell's siege on Paris in the twenties. Her fancy dress parties, come-as-you-are parties, treasure hunts calling for Mistinguett's left slipper, parties on buses outfitted with cocktail bars, parties on a boat with Stavros Niarchos disguised as bartender, a bucolic party where wooden cows gave whiskey and champagne instead of milk, were too much for nearly everyone; except, perhaps, for Arthur Balfour, England's Foreign Minister, who wrote after one such affair to thank her for "the most delightful and degrading" evening.

Eventually the cocktail settled more comfortably into entertainments abroad. Somerset Maugham taught the south of France the rite of making a Martini. The Cole Porters gave "Charleston cocktail parties" with instructions from Bricktop at their home twice a week. Hostess Claudette Colbert elevated rum punch to a position it never relinquished in the Villa Fiorentina at a luau for eighty guests outfitted with sarongs and hibiscus. Ford Madox Ford hosted dancing parties in his studio, enlivened by moonshine imported from America that was

meant to teach Montparnasse the meaning of "likker," but whose effects were not lost on the home team, according to one delighted participant: "whoever has not seen Ezra Pound, ignoring all the rules of tango and of fox-trot, kicking up fantastic heels in a highly personal Charleston, closing his eyes, his toes nimbly scattered right and left, has missed one of the spectacles which reconcile us to life."

By the end of the twenties, the mixed drink was stimulating pre-dinner festivities in France, Italy and Spain, and even across the Channel, where Alec Waugh was by now hosting his own cocktail parties to which "everyone who accepted actually turned up." As of the mid-thirties, "At Home 6:00-8:00" had effectively replaced the after-dinner party in London entertaining and had taken the French avant-garde into the new chic of tiny canapés and alcohol on ice.

Meanwhile, the cocktail party had settled inextricably into American life. It survived the repeal of the amendment that had launched it, by dint of its adaptability, its informality and its unassailable appeal as society's easiest form of entertaining. As it acquired the status of a social institution, the cocktail party moved out from the confines of the city, to ranches and golf courses, to beaches and boat decks, settling into a style of entertaining, both indoors and out, that would remain particularly American.

Those cocktails that had been served wherever people convened—the Tom Collins of Long Island tennis parties, the Gimlets of the racetrack, the fizzes of Bar Harbor regattas, the Stingers of stag nights—were now the acknowledged pretext for gathering people together by engraved invitation. Hosts-with-the-most learned to combine drinks and drinkers for the maximum effect. Whereas the great tables of the past had been commended for their linens, their flatware and the excellence of their wines, these stand-up entertainments were sought out for the celebrity of their guest list and the novelty of their libations. Cocktail society asked nothing more of their hosts than that they provide one golden moment, one instant of froth that, like the cocktail itself, could be sampled immediately and its essence sipped out, before moving on to the next and the next after that.

The new hosts, in turn, asked nothing more than that the key players make an appearance, look glamorous, circulate smoothly and make witty small talk. Success was counted on a scale of numbers and the buzz they created. "Last night I gave a cocktail d'adieu at home and everbody came," crowed cocktail king Noel Coward, whose diaries abound with his triumphs in this venue: "we gave our free for all cocktail party...over fifty came and it was a howling success."

Coward's was a time of snobbery, when it was smart to be seen drinking with society and when everyone wanted to be in the company of the rich and the carefree. A week filled with cocktail parties was reassuring, proof *ne plus ultra* of social distinction, as was the ability to give one in turn that rated a mention in the columns.

Inevitably, such a high note could not be sustained. Albeit well instructed by *Vanity Fair* on how to throw the "ultimate" cocktail party—"a smattering of personalities, plenty of ice and don't forget flowers"—not every social aspirant could muster a Noel Coward first-night guest list, much less mix his "best I

DUBONNET COCKTAIL

Dubonnet is a rich and slightly sweet aperitif wine which was invented in France in 1846. It is best served ice-cold, either straight up in a cordial glass, or in place of vermouth in a cocktail.

To make Noel Coward's favorite Dubonnet Cocktail, combine one ounce of Dubonnet and one ounce of gin in an ice-filled mixing glass. Stir until the mixture is well-chilled, then strain it into a chilled cocktail glass. Garnish with a lemon peel.

have ever tasted I must have another" Dubonnet Cocktail that was the rage that season.

Even as it blossomed into society's most glamorous gathering rite, the cocktail party became vulnerable to the abuses of write-offs and social climbing, gradually losing its appeal. By the sixties it came to be regarded openly as a vehicle for self-promotion and contacts, and little more than a convenient way to gather as many phone numbers as possible. Hostesses now counted their friends in crowds rather than handfuls and became accomplished in introducing guests by profession. The jeweler Kenneth Lane recalls attending one such "purposeful party" at which the hostess, "a young creature fairly new in New York," greeted him effusively at the door, introduced him around the full circuit of two hundred guests and left him back at the door, whereupon he departed, having experienced neither drink nor conversation.

Fortunately, the cocktail itself, sensing endangerment, had long since found a home in every other corner of American conviviality. At the hunt balls of Virginia, Pink Ladies would flow from polished silver stirrup cups. At Jack Warner's Hollywood bashes, champagne would spill from statues of full-breasted nymphs. For Marion Davies' masquerades, rows of cocktail shakers would be lined up along the pool, ready to accommodate as many as two thousand revelers.

Right through the fifties the cocktail graced simple parties and fancy parties, cook-outs and balls. For Frank Sinatra's lavish blasts in Las Vegas, the invitations to which read "Black Tie and Sunglasses," the bartenders were primed with ingredients for the three hundred most popular cocktails of the day. The New

"A GAY, BRIGHT AND BRILLIANT FARCE" RICHARD WATTS

JOHN C. WILSON

PRESENTS

Year's Eve celebrations of Lady Mendl, who had transformed the decor of Manhattan as Elsie de Wolfe, toasted midnight with long flutes of her signature blue cocktails. At Ian Fleming's wedding in Jamaica, the flames of celebration rose from a homemade rum punch, warmly remembered by one of the guests as being set alight to "cheers from the company."

More secure even than its position in calendar festivities was the cocktail's new but inalienable slot in the American day, which was designated by name and by consensus as the happiest of our twenty-four hours. So obvious an assumption would the cocktail hour become that Bernard de Voto could extol it in *The New Yorker* as simply "The Hour." Robert Bench-ley once published a formal request asking "ladies who run tea-rooms not to put signs reading: 'Cocktail Hour' in the windows of their tea-shops at two o'clock in the afternoon. Two P. M. is not 'cocktail hour,' no matter how you look at it. The very suggestion is terrifying."

Some would beg to differ, in accordance with Noel Coward's dictum proclaimed in *The Vortex*: "It's never too early for a cocktail." Harry Truman is remembered for his rejoinder, when denied a Bourbon and Water before the five o'clock opening of a club in Manhattan, "Fine, bring me a drink. It's five o'clock somewhere."

Noon was Hemingway's starting gate; "Past meridien," he would say, "we can break out the serious drinks." Cole Porter, it was humorously alleged, made a custom of turning up at the Ritz bar precisely at noon, dressed in equestrian gear, leaning over to Georges and saying, "Champagne cocktail, please. Had a marvellous ride this morning!" H. L. Mencken, in his own words, "made it a rule, never to drink by daylight and to never refuse a drink after dark." In more recent times a felicitous designation was prefixed to promote what would be officially bannered in establishments across the country as "Happy Hour," a time slot now generously extended to accommodate that suspended period between tea time and dinner.

Thus did cocktails become a national habit and so valued a rite of the civilized world that by the fifties "Come by for cocktails" was the most customary invitation to a gathering. Throughout heartland America mixed drinks took their place in round-the-calendar celebrations: the grogs of Thanksgiving, the Tom and Jerrys of Christmas, the egg nogs of New Year's, the champagne of weddings and all the cocktails of the rainbow for that by now indispensable ritual, the cocktail party.

THE RETURN OF THE COCKTAIL

"Cocktails are society's most enduring invention."
—Elsa Maxwell

Revered in the Gilded Age, energized in the Jazz Age, glamorized in the thirties, ritualized in the forties and incorporated in the fifties, the cocktail met the sixties with the here-to-stay confidence of Babe Ruth at bat. The next two decades saw it nearly strike out. The more intricate confections first faltered when upstairs lost downstairs and one-time matrons of leisure had to cook family dinner. The bottom dropped out of style as the Martini that Dad mixed wearily after his commute from the office was downed on the run between setting the table and eating the roast. Then, just as the timer oven and frozen dinners rescued the cocktail hour, the cocktail itself collided with half-formed theories of physical fitness. In the name of nutrition, spirts were diluted into fruit slushes more suited to the soda fountain than the cocktail lounge, and white wine was substituted before dinner in the mistaken belief that, serving for serving, a glass of wine contains fewer calories and less alcohol than a highball.

Then, somewhere in the seventies, like an urbanite back from a long country weekend, the cocktail returned from its exile in the pale world of very white wine, unpacked all its finery and stepped out on the town in high heels and hip company. Random indications, like the first shoots of spring, signalled its comeback. The burgeoning disco scene promoted exotic mixed drinks as companions to all-night entertainment. Creative bartenders were presenting delicious new drinks incorporating virtuous ingredients like cranberry and grapefruit juice in the instantly popular Sea Breeze, Madras and Greyhound. The annual parties of the Texas Martini Foundation swelled to

bashes of up to three thousand in every major city of the Lone Star State. Across the nation the Sheraton Hotels inaugurated their practice of serving welcome drinks to guests signing in.

In New York socialite Nan Kempner was successfully raising money for the American Ballet Theater by a new chic of "Intermission Cocktail Parties" between acts. The White House, too, added its measure, as First Lady Nancy Reagan reassured the survivors of the parched Carter years that mixed drinks would be served in the White House again.

Cocktails at home stole the limelight as word got around that people were mixing up drinks again. In Manhattan, designer Bill Blass was stirring up a basil and lemon-spiked Danish Mary, mixed and chilled ahead of time according to his high-fashion statement that "like a perfect martini, it's never served on the rocks." In Tobago photographer Norman Parkinson was treating his guests to his special version of a Rum and Ting, while across the Caribbean in Jamaica visitors to Baron Heinrich von Thyssen's tropical Alligator Head House experienced a "rare banana rum punch," named the Saidi after its illustrious inventor, the magnate's majordomo. Meanwhile, Paris model Lulu de la Falaise was introducing the fashion world to her Vampagne: "just add a splash of frozen vodka to champagne and wait to see what happens."

No one is quite certain what turned the tide. Perhaps it was an uprising of restless palates bored with indifferent white wines, led by food critics who, observing the proliferation of ethnic foods, note that flavorful mixed drinks stand up better to spices than even premium wines; perhaps the dread of loss that strikes when anything finely crafted is threatened with

TEQUILA SUNRISE
The Tequila Sunrise, so named for the drink's rosy orange glow, was one of the first cocktails to popularize tequila, in California and later throughout the United States.

Combine a shot of tequila with orange juice over ice in a collins glass or goblet. Float a dash of grenadine on top, and garnish with orange and a cherry. The Rolling Stones introduced a version of the Tequila Sunrise containing two shots of tequila which they called, inexplicably, an "In Drink."

183

SEA BREEZE, BAY BREEZE
AND CAPE CODDER

America's fascination with both cranberry juice and vodka has led to the invention of these cool and refreshing cocktails. All three begin with a shot of vodka over ice in a collins glass. For a Cape Codder, simply fill with cranberry juice. For a Sea Breeze, top with cranberry juice and a generous splash of grapefruit juice; for a Bay Breeze, it's cranberry and pineapple juice, in the same proportions as in a Sea Breeze.

extinction. Or possibly it was a twinge of pride, similar to that which the French had always taken in their great wines and fine brandies, for America's ryes and bourbons, now internationally recognized among the world's foremost spirits.

Trendspotters noted a fascination with the style of the thirties and a yearning for all things evocative of the era of cufflinks and ballgowns. The fashion houses of Seventh Avenue first kissed the cheeks with cocktail veils, then rolled down the runway with the short-skirted cocktail dress.

And the New York entertainment establishment followed suit. The "21" Club re-opened, and the Rainbow Room, whose opening-night crowd in October, 1934 included Cole Porter, Elsa Maxwell and Noel Coward, opened it's doors again in 1987, revamped and revitalized to "wed the icon of the thirties to the spirit of the eighties." "It has marked the rites of passage for so many generations," observed club manager Joseph Baum of the tradition in which the Rainbow Room is steeped. David Rockefeller, chairman of Rockefeller Center where the club is located, concurred, recalling the time he and his wife-to-be won a polka contest—first prize having been a turkey which they gave to orchestra leader Ruby Newman—on the original version of the famous revolving dance floor, restored today by a craftsman who's the grandson of the man who installed the original floor in the thirties and the son of the man who refurbished it in the fifties.

Economics also played a part. Budget-conscious hostesses rediscovered that the cocktail party, cleverly styled with butler, canapés and a full bar, could be twice as glamorous as the traditional sit-down dinner, at half the cost. Inescapably, too,

LONG ISLAND ICED TEA
A classic misnomer, Long Island Iced Tea contains no tea, iced or otherwise. Also know as New York Iced Tea, it is made from equal parts of rum, vodka, gin, triple sec, lemon juice, orange juice and cola poured over ice and served in a large collins glass or goblet.

187

MAI TAI

An original invention of the Banyan Tree Hotel in Honolulu, the Mai Tai, like the Daiquiri from Cuba and the Piña Colada from Puerto Rico, was created in the tropics and imported to the U.S. by returning vacationers. It remains a special favorite in Polynesian barstops like Trader Vic's.

The classic Mai Tai combines two shots of light rum, one shot of dark rum, a half shot of Curaçao and a half shot of orgeat in a goblet half filled with crushed ice. Add more ice to bring the drink level to just below the rim and stir gently. Garnish with mint, pineapple, and a cherry.

For a blended Mai Tai, combine half measures of light rum, dark rum, triple sec and tequila with full measures of apricot brandy, orgeat and orange juice in a blender. Add a dash of Angostura bitters and two dashes of grenadine. Blend and serve in a goblet or old-fashioned glass, garnished with fresh fruit.

as the quality of white wine served by the glass decreased in relation to its cost, the young and the wordly, who found themselves paying four dollars for a glass of grape extract harvested that morning, were returning to value-for-money spirits they could rely on.

Fortunately, when these seekers of the good life awoke to the merit of our imperilled national treasure and set off to its rescue, they found cocktails not only alive and unharmed, but comfortably lodged in the very best places where stirred, mixed and shaken, they had been keeping fit and alert for their comeback in the eighties.

Where, then, are they now, the Bronx and the Sidecar? Give or take a few of the more eccentric concoctions that have gone to an oblivion deserved at the time of invention, the very same libations are being served up, where the gods have been kindest, at the very same places and by the identical barmen who had poured them so expertly years before.

In Los Angeles, Francois Mouvet, barkeep of Scandia since 1955, still works his double row of spirits into any one of three hundred cocktail combinations stored in his memory. Twenty years after his fiery debut, Pepe Ruiz continues to heat up the mahogany at Chasen's with his Flame of Love Martini, while at The Palm in West Hollywood twenty-four-year veteran Irv Frost has disciplined himself to keep the tricks out of the classics, guaranteeing regulars like Joe Namath "some constants in this changing world." More willing to experiment is Gus Tassopulos, who placed celebrities' orders on the rocks at the Beverly Hills Polo Lounge for more than a quarter century and is now serving their progeny at Mason's with a new repertoire;

rum punches, Piña Coladas and Strawberry Daiquiris, which are "more fun for the young, though when they hit the more formal establishments it's back to Mother's Martinis and Dad's Scotch on the Rocks." The track record to beat in the West is that of Valerio Batugo who, after an incredible forty years, is still stirring things up at Tips in Anaheim with inventions like the Universe, a stellar mix of Suntory Old, Midori, vodka and Pistasche liqueur. "You've got to keep your hand in," says this spiritous patriarch of his most recent invention, the multi-hued Twinkling Star that orbits around rum, blue Curaçao, sabayon and three juices.

Keeping their hands in along the barfronts of Manhattan are a tribe of professionals who have been cradling the classics for comeback day. "You wouldn't believe how my Martinis are selling again," beams Henry Milke, long-time barkeep of The Four Seasons. "Nothing out of date about the Old Fashioned," chuckles Charlie Clarke, who has served them up at P. J. Clarke's since today's cocktail crowd was knee high to a Grasshopper. "If you wait long enough, everything comes full circle," says Mose Perracchio, who has reigned at the Oak Bar for forty years, of the Whiskey Sour that earlier gladtimers had rated the best in town and that the vodka generation is starting to take up again.

Intriguingly, there is hardly an old-style drink that hasn't its showplace on the contemporary scene. Care for a Stinger? At New York's Carlton House this graceful after-dinner drink is mixed to perfection with imported crème de menthe and the finest French brandy. How about a Mint Julep? Washington's Willard Hotel still offers this taste of the Old South, as charm-

SINGAPORE SLING

The Singapore Sling was invented at the Raffles Hotel in Singapore, and provided not a small part of the island's attraction for the likes of Somerset Maugham, Joseph Conrad and Douglas Fairbanks. It is a delightful companion to any summertime occasion, its vivid color and refreshing cool an instant passage to the enjoyable lull of the tropics.

The Raffles Hotel recipe calls for a shot of gin, a shot of cherry brandy, a teaspoon of sugar, the juice of half a lemon and a dash of bitters, all combined over ice in a collins glass, topped with soda and garnished with lemon, orange and a cherry. Variations allow for a shot of sloe gin or apricot brandy, a dash of port wine, Benedictine, Drambuie or grenadine, and the substitution of ginger ale for soda.

ing as the one Senator Henry Clay first mixed there. Crave an old-fashioned punch? The Hotel Carlyle's Bemelmans Bar claims a recipe involving brandy and champagne that dates from pre-war Baden-Baden. Fancy an authentic Margarita? Tequila fans say that its stellar performance at the Arizona Inn is what earned Tucson's charming resort a coveted fourth star. At Savannah's Shrimp Factory you can inhale in a snifter the very same union of rye, rum, gin, brandy, tea, orange and lemon juice that fortified President Monroe on the occasion of the launching of the SS *Savannah*. At the Breakers Hotel in Palm Beach the thirties come alive in the classic reconstruction of the champagne-and-orange-juice Mimosa, now popular once again. To this day Boston's best-known Martini, stirred precisely twelve times, resides at the Ritz Carlton Bar, where the waiters continue to mix drinks on their trays.

Even more gratifying to the liquid archeologist is the number of sites still in the business of serving up the confections to which they gave birth. A spirited tour of original watering holes might begin with Honolulu's Banyan Tree Bar, birthplace of the Mai Tai, proceed to the legendary Antoine's in New Orleans, which still enacts the ritual of dimming the lights when a flaming Café Brulot is served, cross over to the Thistle Lodge Restaurant in Sanibel, Florida to re-enact chef Peter Harman's eureka discovery of the Cajun Margarita, then head up the coast to Manhattan and the Waldorf Astoria, where the legendary Johnny Solon invented the Bronx. After journeying over to London for a stop at the Savoy Hotel for Peter Dorelli's presentation of a White Lady as pristine as she was the day

MADRAS

Another product of the recent popularity of cranberry juice, a properly prepared Madras should resemble its namesake fabric, a brightly-colored cotton from the state of Madras in India.

To an ice-filled highball or old-fashioned glass, add an ounce and a half of vodka. Fill with orange juice until drink level is just below the rim. Slowly drip cranberry juice around the inside edge so that it makes red streaks in the drink. Do not stir.

Harry Craddock invented her there, one might take the Concorde on a fling for a Sling in Singapore at the Raffles Bar, whose seemingly peripheral position on the cocktail circuit has never daunted the faithful.

One suspects that part of the cocktail's appeal for a society on the move is its wanderlust. Uninhibited by the delicate constitutions of vintage wines, liquor travels well and extensively. There are no limits to where a good drink can lead: to the Left Bank's Closerie des Lilas, whose art deco mirrors frame Claude's lauded Martinis; to Rome's Grand Hotel, whose arch-bibulous have named Mauro Lotti the finest barlord in Italy for his stewardship of his *cavalli di battaglia*, his warhorses—the Martini, the Manhattan, and the Daiquiri; on to Harry's Bar in Venice, still afloat in expatriates, to requite the nostalgia for the world's first Bloody Mary; to London for the lunchtime Pimm's that barman Harry Adams has been confecting since the thirties at Simpson's Smoking Room Bar; north to Copenhagen and the sybaritic refuge of the Plaza Hotel's Library Bar, to surrender to leather armchairs and the legendary house nightcap built on Kahlua, Cognac and freshly-brewed coffee.

Ironically, while the rest of the world prides itself on maintaining the traditions of the American bar, America's bars have been exploring more innovative venues. Once word got about that cocktails were back in style, newer establishments angled for a piece of the crowd with provocative theme drinks like the Dive Bomber of the Pilot's Grill Restaurant in Bangor, Maine and the Sex on the Beach at Nicky Blair's of West Hollywood, and with eye-catching designer drinks like Pat O'Brien's five-color Separators.

The more aggressive developed signature drinks as palatable ways to promote their own names. Thus a Stars Martini, developed by Jeremiah Tower's Stars Restaurant in San Francisco, makes the classic its own by substituting tequila for vermouth and garnishing with lime. Manhattan's Hotel Parker Meridien packs a Parker Punch with Jamaica rum and a combination of fresh juices spritzed with club soda. Mad Anthony's, a Pennsylvania bar that is proclaimed to be haunted, has devised the Mad Anthony from four kinds of whiskey, which it claims steadies the customers when the poltergeists take over. Duke Macks, an enterprising "We never close" eatery on Atlantic City's Boardwalk, pulls them in with the Dirty Duke and the Mack Attack, then sends them on their way with the hurricane glasses in which these inspirations are served. In Tulsa, Oklahoma, the Excelsior Hotel promotes its Rattlesnake Excelsior in "homeopathic doses," claiming this elixir of rye whiskey, Pernod, powdered ginger, egg white and lemon juice "aids digestion, acts antihistimatically on colds, slaughters flu germs, relieves headaches and wears the warts off the spirit."

Enterprising bartenders of the new school are currently enlivening the cocktail scene with eclectic contributions like the Survival Smog with which bartender Jack Martin keeps the air sweet at Morton's in Los Angeles. The technicolor dazzlers streaming out of Pat O'Brien's in New Orleans contribute to its claim of most spirits sold at a single location—the Blue Tail Fly, the Cyclone and barkeep Cheryl Markward's Rainbow, a flag-waving combination of red grenadine, white grain spirits, blue Curaçao and collins mix, all served up in tall, crested glasses reading "Have Fun."

If no one takes these contrivances seriously, that's okay by management, whose operating principle is spirited conviviality. Rusty Staub's alert establishment in Manhattan encourages consumer participation with a five-dollar offer to "Make Your Own Drink" from an impressive display of exotic new liqueurs that are undeniably vivid, if egregiously sweet.

While generously acknowledging the supremacy of the classics, none of the newer establishments has shied from the ices and creams that inspired the soda fountain drinks of the sixties. Rather, there has been a self-confessed effort to create sweet, liquid entremets for that majority of Americans who never order desserts in restaurants. The resulting confections are proving predictably popular and pulling the cocktail into an even sweeter realm of entertainment. Mom's Strawberry Shortcake, which conceals amaretto and brandy under fresh fruit and cream, is the big draw at Oscar's in Tempe, Arizona. The Shallows in Fort Myers, Florida courts the sweet tooth with Frozen Key Lime Pie, and Carlucci's in Chicago is doing brisk business with its trademark Frozen Cappucino, a luscious alliance of whipped cream, chocolate milk, hazelnut liqueur and, last but least, coffee.

In this contemporary conviction, resurrected from the thirties, that a cocktail can be a mini-barrel of fun, the livelier gathering places are minting libations that generate an atmosphere of play and good times. First to let their frolicsome new drinks cavort among the classics have been the holiday playgrounds, the sunspots that cater to the overheated with cool fruity enticements named for anything attention-getting, like the Marvy Surfbangers that are keeping the beaches of Waikiki

clement, or the Kiss Me Again that is blowing the breeze in Palm Beach. The winter resorts administer northern comfort with reviving warm alcohols, artful concoctions like the Sierra, created originally for the local ski team out of Tia Maria, Frangelica and brandy by Chuck Barondess of Zeke's in Denver, Colorado. At Sugarloaf, Maine's lively alpine resort, locals stop in at Gepetto's for the zest that Slippery Nipples bring to the downhill experience. Telluride, Colorado, boasting a population of 1,200 and twelve bars on its Main Street, warms the after-ski crowd on hot toddies and shooters with names like B52 and Skip and Go Naked. The good-time formula in Dallas inaugurates the evening at the Filling Station with a Tune Up of gin and blue Curaçao, proceeds to Reunion Tower for Texas Twisters and spins on to Studebakers, to take off with Bailey's Comet.

Even cocktails at home have taken a new turn. "Come by for cocktails" is competing with the lately-fashionable invitation to drop in for tea. Vintage stores are reporting a run on art deco shakers, and Bloomingdale's now carries eight different kinds of martini glasses, as serving pre-dinner cocktails has flowered into a time-affordable, cost-compatible yet highly fashionable way to entertain friends.

Drinking patterns have changed. Inclined toward moderation, society no longer looks tolerantly on excess; spirits are now the symbol, not the source of American conviviality. Nor is it likely that Prohibition will ever again exert its chokehold. Cocktails will remain one of this culture's most persistent pleasures, the first ceremony at day's end, just as spirits will continue

200

to be associated cheerfully with those holidays and celebrations and affairs of the heart that are too meaningful for the decanting of a bottle of water.

Inviting and flavorful, the cocktail has taken its place in the world of design and gourmet imbibing. At once styled and stylish, formal and adaptable, it is a viable part of a society in motion, a high-spirited contributor and graceful complement to the emergent good life. Easily accommodated by the spin of an egg white to nouvelle cuisine or by the trick of three juices to a fitness regime, the cocktail is welcomed as it circles the globe speaking to the world in a liquid esperanto confected from the aromatic rums of the Indies, the pungent malts of Scotland and the cool, blue-neon liqueurs of Paris after-hours.

Heightening its appeal for a do-it-yourself society is the knowledge that anyone can make a contemporary classic. True, there is a measure of discipline involved—"Cocktails demand concentration," as cosmopolite Isabelle Goldsmith has observed—but the rewards of creative mixology are immediate. A good cocktail, perfectly prepared and stylishly presented, will make a long evening shorter and a good dinner better, binding people together in a warm rite of comradeship as they joyously celebrate the life of the spirit. So in the new spirit of harmony, moderation and immeasurable style, let us celebrate America's liquid icon: long may the water of life, the fruit of the earth and their sublime fermentations combine into that blithest of all spirits. Here's to the Cocktail—cheers, *prosit*, *skaal*, *salud* and may it enjoy health and prosperity for one hundred thousand years!

CREDITS

Photography was shot in Los Angeles and Washington, D.C. Baccarat provided crystal for both locations; additional crystal was provided for the Washington photography by Toscany, Sasaki and Rogaska. Lindsay Fontana coordinated photography in Los Angeles, with Norman Stewart, food stylist, and Cassandra Einstein, prop stylist. In Washington, Dennis Roche of the Roche Salon and Yvonne Creighton served as hair and make-up stylists, Nancy Lendved as prop stylist, and Pascale Lemaire as clothing stylist. Appreciation also goes to Monica Quagliotti and Range Rover of North America, Inc., to Natasha Reatig and to Mike Wilson.

The publisher would also like to thank the following people and organizations for their courteous and generous assistance in providing locations, props and materials for the photography in the book.

Page 2 Blithe Spirit - Photograph by Jesse Gerstein. Location: Hotel Bel Air, Los Angeles. Crystal: *Marennes*, by Baccarat.

Page 6 Photograph by Mark Daniels. Models: Dana and Jerome Adamstein.

Pages 8-9 Texas Fizz - Photograph by Jesse Gerstein. Location: Hotel Bel Air, Los Angeles. Crystal: *Orion*, by Baccarat.

Page 10 Stinger - Photograph by Jesse Gerstein. Location: Home of Nancy Lendved, Washington, D.C. Crystal: *Wyndam*, by Toscany. Chess set from Camalier and Buckley, Washington, D.C; pipe from Georgetown Tobacco, Washington, D.C.

Page 14 Gin Rickey - Photograph by Jesse Gerstein. Location: Studio of Sharon Truax, Venice, California. Crystal: *Nancy*, by Baccarat. Siphon from Gumps, Beverly Hills.

Page 18 Between the Sheets - Photograph by Jesse Gerstein. Location: Hollyhock House. Hollyhock House is owned by the City of Los Angeles and operated by the Cultural Affairs Department. Crystal: *Perfection*, by Baccarat.

Page 21 Tamara Cocktail - Photograph by Jesse Gerstein. Location: Home of Nancy Lendved, Washington, D.C. Crystal: *Tucano*, by Sasaki.

Page 22 Daiquiri - Photograph by Jesse Gerstein. Location: 72 Market Street Oyster Bar and Grill, Los Angeles. Wooden railing by Bill Tunberg.

Page 25 Daiquiri - Photograph by Mark Daniels. Crystal: *Perfection*, by Baccarat.

Page 26 Rum Label from The Seagram Museum, Waterloo, Ontario.

Page 28 Matchcover from Bill Retskin of The Front Striker, Alexandria, Virginia.

Page 29 Cuba Libre - Photograph by Jesse Gerstein. Location: Studio and collection of Sharon Truax, Venice, California.

Page 31 Old Fashioned - Photograph by Jesse Gerstein. Location: Biltmore Hotel, Los Angeles. Crystal: *Rotary*, by Baccarat. Tray by Tiffany & Co., Beverly Hills.

Page 33 Whisky Advertisement from The Seagram Museum, Waterloo, Ontario.

Page 34 Seven and Seven, Bloody Mary - Photograph by Mark Daniels. Location: Paper Chase Farms, Middleburg, Virginia. Range Rover courtesy of Range Rover of North America, Inc.; picnic basket from Camalier & Buckley, Washington, D.C. Models: Grace Broderick, Lori Yaag and John Rusnak.

Page 35 Seven and Seven - Photograph by Jesse Gerstein. Location: Martha Bodman Lefkovits, ISID Interior Design, Los Angeles. Crystal: *Harmonie*, by Baccarat.

Page 36 Gin Advertisement from The Seagram Museum, Waterloo, Ontario.

Page 38 Salty Dog - Photograph by Jesse Gerstein. Location: Home of Jan and Edward Woods; Architect, Mulder-Katkov, Venice, California. Crystal: *Nancy*, by Baccarat.

Pages 40-41 Moscow Mule - Photograph by Jesse Gerstein. Location: Hollyhock House. Hollyhock House is owned by the City of Los Angeles and operated by the Cultural Affairs Department.

Page 41 Moscow Mule - Photograph by Mark Daniels. Location: Tabard Inn, Washington, D.C. Model: John Rusnak.

Page 42 Photograph by Mark Daniels. Crystal: *Perfection*, by Baccarat. Model: Connie Jean Dolinger.

Page 43 Vodka Label from The Seagram Museum, Waterloo, Ontario.

Page 45 Blithe Spirit - Photograph by Mark Daniels. Models: Viktor Valentine and Shelley Waitt.

Page 46 Champagne Label from The Seagram Museum, Waterloo, Ontario.

Page 47 Matchcover from Bill Retskin of The Front Striker, Alexandria, Virginia.

Page 48 Bellini - Photograph by Mark Daniels. Location: Stonyhurst, Middleburg, Virginia. Glasses from Bellinis, New York City. Models: Laurie Pettigrew and Ben Wartofsky.

Page 49 Bellini - Photograph by Jesse Gerstein. Location: Home of Nancy Lendved, Washington, D.C. Glasses from Bellinis, New York City.

Page 51 Margarita - Photograph by Jesse Gerstein. Location: Home of Jill Spalding, Los Angeles. Margarita set by Dorothy Thorpe, from Thanks for the Memories, Los Angeles.

Page 52 Tequila Label from Seagram Museum, Waterloo, Ontario.

Page 53 Margarita - Photograph by Mark Daniels. Location: Tabard Inn, Washington, D.C.

Page 54 Photograph by Mark Daniels. Model: Barbara Bien.

Pages 56-57 Americano - Photograph by Jesse Gerstein. Location: Al Gelato Continental Desserts & Cafe, Los Angeles. Crystal: *Athena*, by Baccarat.

Page 58 Brandy Alexander - Photograph by Jesse Gerstein. Location: Collection of Douglas Bergeron, Los Angeles. Crystal: *Genova*, by Baccarat.

Page 59 Brandy Alexander - Photograph by Mark Daniels. Crystal: *Genova*, by Baccarat. Model: Michèle A. Pereira.

Page 61 Rusty Nail - Photograph by Jesse Gerstein. Location: Studio of Sharon Truax, Venice, California. Crystal: *Pluton*, by Baccarat.

Page 62 Cognac Label from The Seagram Museum, Waterloo, Ontario.

Page 63 Cognac - Photograph by Mark Daniels. Models: Elva Anderson and Joseph Beckford

Page 64 Crème de Menthe Frappe - Photograph by Jesse Gerstein. Location: Collection of Douglas Bergeron, Los Angeles.

Page 67 Crème de Menthe Frappe - Photograph by Mark Daniels. Location: Pisces Club, Washington, D.C. Dresses from Sonja's Boutique, Columbia, Maryland. Suits from Hyatt & Co., Columbia, Maryland. Models: Jeff Skeen, Hallie Bonnell, Daniel Coiner, Mary Lynne Henry, Terry Groman and Elaine Roecklein.

Page 68 Mint Julep - Photograph by Jesse Gerstein. Location: Hotel Bel Air, Los Angeles. Tray from Tiffany & Co., Beverly Hills. Cups from Gumps, Beverly Hills.

Page 71 Bloody Mary - Photograph by Jesse Gerstein. Location: Home of Jill Spalding. Crystal: *Athena*, by Baccarat. Silver spoon and tongs from Tiffany & Co., Beverly Hills.

Pages 72-73 Champagne Cocktail - Photograph by Jesse Gerstein. Location: Hotel Queen Mary, Long Beach, California. Crystal: *Massena*, by Baccarat. Mask by Marga, Los Angeles.

Page 74 "Gin" Dispensing Barrel (England, c.1890) from The Seagram Museum, Waterloo, Ontario.

Page 75 Miniature Bottles (20th Century) from The Seagram Museum, Waterloo, Ontario.

Page 77 Martini - Photograph by Mark Daniels. Location: Pisces Club, Washington, D.C. Woman's Suit from Sonja's Boutique, Columbia, Maryland. Models: Hallie Bonnell and Daniel Coiner.

Page 79 Martini - Photograph by Jesse Gerstein. Location: Home of Nancy Lendved, Washington, D.C. Crystal: *Spectrum*, by Toscany.

Page 80 Manhattan - Photograph by Jesse Gerstein. Location: Collection of Douglas Bergeron, Los Angeles.

Page 81 Photograph by Mark Daniels. Models: David Del Monte.

Page 82 Blue Hawaiian - Photograph by Jesse Gerstein. Location: Rebecca's Restaurant, Venice, California. Crystal: *Pavillion*, by Baccarat; Sculpture: *Pensée*, by Baccarat.

Page 83 Blue Hawaiian - Photograph by Mark Daniels. Crystal: *Perfection*, by Baccarat. Model: Patty Prendergast.

Page 84 Whiskey Sour - Photograph by Mark Daniels. Location: Pisces Club, Washington, D.C. Dress from Sonja's Boutique, Columbia, Maryland. Suit from Hyatt & Co., Columbia, Maryland. Models: Elaine Roecklein and Terry Groman.

Page 86 Whiskey Sour - Photograph by Jesse Gerstein. Location: 72 Market Street Oyster Bar and Grill, Los Angeles. Chairs by Jacky Pecheron.

Page 88 Irish Coffee - Photograph by Mark Daniels. Location: Tabard Inn, Washington, D.C. Models: Barry Dixon and John Rusnak.

Pages 88-89 Irish Coffee - Photograph by Jesse Gerstein. Location: Hotel Queen Mary, Long Beach, California. Coffee pot, mugs and spoon from Tiffany & Co., Beverly Hills.

Page 91 Rob Roy - Photograph by Jesse Gerstein. Location: Home of Nancy Lendved, Washington, D.C. Crystal: *Spectrum*, by Toscany. Leather books from Lori Ponder Ltd., Washington, D.C.

Page 92 Gimlet - Photograph by Jesse Gerstein. Location: Home of Jill Spalding, Los Angeles. Martini glasses by Dorothy Thorpe, from Thanks for the Memories, Los Angeles.

Page 95 Gimlet - Photograph by Mark Daniels. Location: Tabard Inn, Washington, D.C. Models: Barry Dixon and Rebecca Peed.

Page 99 Top Banana - Photograph by Jesse Gerstein. Location: Home of Shelley Menning; Architect, Brian Murphy. Crystal from Gumps, Beverly Hills.

Page 100 Sidecar - Photograph by Jesse Gerstein. Location: Home of Jan and Edward Woods; Architect, Mulder-Katkov, Venice, California. Crystal: *Perfection*, by Baccarat.

Pages 104-105 Black Russian - Photograph by Mark Daniels. Crystal: *Mercure*, by Baccarat.

Page 106 Black Russian - Photograph by Jesse Gerstein. Location: Home of Shelley Menning; Architect, Brian Murphy. Crystal: *Mercure*, by Baccarat.

Page 108 Photograph of Winston Churchill from Magnum Photos, Inc.

Page 110 Sazerac - Photograph by Mark Daniels. Location: Tabard Inn, Washington, D.C. Model: Barry Dixon.

Page 111 Sazerac - Photograph by Jesse Gerstein. Location: A Home in Venice, California.

Page 113 Photograph of Ernest Hemingway from Globe Photos, Inc.

Page 115 Kir Royale - Photograph by Jesse Gerstein. Location: Rex, Il Ristorante, Los Angeles. Crystal: *Dom Pérignon*, by Baccarat.

Page 116 Sloe Gin Fizz - Crystal: *Perfection*, by Baccarat. Model: Connie Jean Dolinger.

Page 117 Sloe Gin Fizz - Photograph by Jesse Gerstein. Location: Home of Jan and Edward Woods; Architect, Mulder-Katkov, Venice, California.

Page 118 Grasshopper - Photograph by Jesse Gerstein. Location: Rex, Il Ristorante, Los Angeles. Crystal by Lalique and silver tray, from Tiffany & Co., Beverly Hills.

Page 119 Grasshopper - Photograph by Mark Daniels. Location: Pisces Club, Washington, D.C. Crystal: *Renaissance Gold*, by Sasaki. Dress from Austin Mace, Takoma Park, Maryland. Model: Hallie Bonnell.

Pages 120-121 Ramos Fizz - Photograph by Jesse Gerstein. Location: Hotel Bel Air, Los Angeles. Crystal: *St. Remy*, by Baccarat. Vase: *Cyclades*, by Baccarat.

Page 122 Bel Air Royale - Photograph by Jesse Gerstein. Location: Hotel Bel Air, Los Angeles.

Page 124 Bel Air Royale - Photograph by Mark Daniels. Location: Tabard Inn, Washington, D.C. Silver bud vase and butter plate courtesy of Two Lions Antiques & Interiors, Washington, D.C.. Pillows, tray, china and butter knife from the collection of Christopher and Lisa Rasmussen Smith, Washington, D.C. Model: Rebecca Peed.

Page 126 "Brandy" Spirit Flagon (England, c. 1880) from The Seagram Museum, Waterloo, Ontario.

Page 129 Tom Collins - Photograph by Mark Daniels. Crystal: *Rotary*, by Baccarat.

Page 130 Tom Collins - Photograph by Jesse Gerstein. Location: Studio of Sharon Truax, Venice, California. Crystal from Tiffany & Co., Beverly Hills.

Page 132 Planter's Punch - Photograph by Mark Daniels. Location: Home of Lydia Gillman, Purcellville, Virginia. Model: Grace Broderick and Jack.

Page 135 Planter's Punch - Photograph by Jesse Gerstein. Location: Rebecca's Restaurant, Venice, California. Crystal: *Paris*, by Baccarat.

Pages 136-137 Pink Lady - Photograph by Mark Daniels. Model: Jan Drezo.

Page 139 Pink Lady - Photograph by Jesse Gerstein. Location: Collection of Douglas Bergeron, Los Angeles.

Page 141 Matchcover from Bill Retskin of The Front Striker, Alexandria, Virginia

Page 145 Clover Club - Photograph by Jesse Gerstein. Location: Biltmore Hotel, Los Angeles. Crystal: *Paris*, by Baccarat. Compact from Tiffany & Co., Beverly Hills.

Page 146 Matchcover from Bill Retskin of The Front Striker, Alexandria, Virginia

Page 149 Photograph courtesy of Club El Morocco.

Page 150 Photograph courtesy of Club El Morocco.

Page 151 Matchcover from Bill Retskin of The Front Striker, Alexandria, Virginia

Pages 152-153 Pimm's Cup - Photograph by Jesse Gerstein. Location: Hotel Bel Air, Los Angeles. Crystal from Gumps, Beverly Hills.

Page 157 Piña Colada - Photograph by Mark Daniels. Location: Tabard Inn, Washington, D.C. Models: Diane Gleason and Scott McDonald.

Page 158 Piña Colada - Photograph by Jesse Gerstein. Location: Hotel Bel Air, Los Angeles.

Page 161 Set of Excise Spirit Measures (England or Ireland, c. 1850) from The Seagram Museum, Waterloo, Ontario.

Page 162 Pousse Cafe - Photograph by Jesse Gerstein. Location: Hotel Bel Air, Los Angeles.

Page 165 Pousse Cafe - Photograph by Mark Daniels. Location: CITIES, Washington, D.C. Clothes from Cignal (Georgetown), Washington, D.C.; black dress by Pascale Lemaire. Models: Alexandre von Furstenberg, Cameil White, Joaquin Rodriguez.

Page 167 Wine Decanting Device from The Seagram Museum, Waterloo, Ontario.

Pages 168-169 Tom and Jerry - Photograph by Jesse Gerstein. Location: Hotel Bel Air, Los Angeles. Silver Tray by Tiffany & Co., Beverly Hills. Napkins from Gumps, Beverly Hills. Flowers by Sharon Truax, Venice, California. Cookies by Rosemary Hardesty.

Page 171 Photograph by Mark Daniels. Crystal: *Rotary*, by Baccarat. Models: Kimberly Lura and Cyrus Chamberlain.

Page 177 Dubonnet Cocktail - Photograph by Jesse Gerstein. Location: Hotel Bel Air, Los Angeles. Crystal from Gumps, Beverly Hills. Sculpture: *Sirius*, by Baccarat. Cigarette case & lighter, silver picture frame, ashtray and pen from Tiffany & Co., Beverly Hills.

Page 179 Blown, Pressed and Moulded Bar Tumblers (1820-1890) from The Seagram Museum, Waterloo, Ontario.

Page 180 Tequila Sunrise - Photograph by Jesse Gerstein. Location: Home of Nancy Lendved, Washington, D.C. Crystal: *Casablanca*, by Sasaki.

Page 182 Tequila Sunrise - Photograph by Mark Daniels. Location: Home of Lydia Gillman, Purcellville, Virginia. Towel from Hecht's, Arlington, Virginia. Models: Laurie Pettigrew, Grace Broderick and Etta Trix.

Pages 184-185 Sea Breeze, Cape Codder and Bay Breeze - Photograph by Jesse Gerstein. Location: Home of Nancy Lendved, Washington, D.C. Crystal: *Direction*, by Toscany.

Page 186 Long Island Iced Tea - Photograph by Jesse Gerstein. Location: Home of Mr. and Mrs. Julio Wahl.

Page 189 Mai Tai - Photograph by Mark Daniels. Location: Home of Lydia Gillman, Purcellville, Virginia. Models: Jim Yates, John Rusnak, Laurie Pettigrew, Lori Yaag, Grace Broderick, Ben Wartofsky.

Page 190 Mai Tai - Photograph by Jesse Gerstein. Location: A Home in Rustic Canyon, California. Crystal: *Mercure*, by Baccarat. Flowers by Sharon Truax, Venice, California.

Page 192 Singapore Sling - Photograph by Jesse Gerstein. Location: Collection of Douglas Bergeron, Los Angeles. Crystal: *Rotary*, by Baccarat.

Page 193 Singapore Sling - Photograph by Mark Daniels. Location: CITIES, Washington, D.C. Glassware from Cafe Lautrec, Washington, D.C. Clothes from Urban Outfitters and Cignal (Georgetown), Washington, D.C. Models: Alexandre von Furstenberg, Cameil White, Jeff Skeen and Joaquin Rodriguez.

Pages 194-195 Madras - Photograph by Jesse Gerstein. Location: Home of Nancy Lendved, Washington, D.C. Crystal: *Marina*, by Rogaska.

Page 199 Sex on the Beach - Photograph by Jesse Gerstein. Location: Home and collection of Nancy Lendved, Washington, D.C.

INDEX

207